KU-479-993

Disney

Christmas
Storybook
Collection

700034344474

Christmas
Storybook
Collection

This book belongs to

....

This edition published by Parragon in 2013
Parragon
Chartist House
15–17 Trim Street
Bath BA1 1HA, UK
www.parragon.com

Copyright © 2013 Disney Enterprises, Inc.
Copyright © 2013 Disney/Pixar
101 Dalmatians based on the book The Hundred and One Dalmatians by Dodie Smith,
published by The Viking Press
Winnie the Pooh based on the 'Winnie the Pooh' works by A.A. Milne and E.H. Shepard

All rights reserved. No part of this publication may be reproduced, stored in a retrieval
system or transmitted, in any form or by any means, electronic, mechanical, photocopying,
recording or otherwise, without the prior permission of the copyright holder.

ISBN 978-1-4723-1877-0

Printed in China

Christmas
Storybook
Collection

Bath · New York · Singapore · Hong Kong · Cologne · Delhi
Melbourne · Amsterdam · Johannesburg · Shenzhen

Contents

The Perfect Gift

Christmas was just a few days away. Geppetto, the old wood-carver, was busy making toy soldiers and pretty dolls for the boys and girls in the village. There seemed to be more toys than usual to make this year. Geppetto was afraid that he wouldn't get all the work done in time.

Geppetto's son, Pinocchio, was eager to help his father. He knew that Geppetto worked harder during the Christmas season than at any other time of the year. While Geppetto worked day and night to make all the toys, Pinocchio, with the help of Jiminy Cricket, decorated the house for the holidays. They put up a tree and strung popcorn on its branches and they hung garlands of holly.

This would be Pinocchio's first Christmas as a real boy, so he wanted it to be very special.

"Jiminy," Pinocchio said, "I want to find the perfect gift for Geppetto. He should have something special. Will you help me?"

"Hmm," Jiminy said. "Well, if you ask me—"

"Maybe he would like a new knife to carve with?" Pinocchio said. He thought that he might not have enough money for that. "Oh, what about some warm gloves? He could use them when he goes out on cold nights to deliver toys."

"You know, Pinocchio, I wonder if a better gift would be—" Jiminy began.

"Socks!" Pinocchio cried. "Or a new hat! Come on, Jiminy, let's go to the shops and see what we can find." Pinocchio hurried out of the door. Jiminy had to run to keep up.

In the shops, Pinocchio looked at socks, warm hats, gloves, scarves and even a warm woollen coat. Everything was too small, too expensive, or too ordinary. Pinocchio wanted to find something special.

By Christmas Eve, Pinocchio still hadn't found the perfect gift for Geppetto. He felt sad.

"What am I going to do?" he asked Jiminy.

"Well, I do have this idea," the cricket said.

"Really?" Pinocchio asked. "Please tell me!"

Jiminy sat him at the table and handed him a quill pen.

"You want to give your father something he really needs?"

"I sure do." Pinocchio beamed.

"Write this," Jiminy said.

"'Dear Geppetto, my gift to you is an extra pair of hands and an extra-willing heart. Love, Pinocchio.'"

When Pinocchio finished writing, he looked up at Jiminy. "Now what?" he asked.

"Now, you put the note in here." Jiminy held out a box. Pinocchio dropped the note in. Then, Jiminy wrapped the package with bright paper and a big bow.

"Geppetto will be very happy with this gift," Jiminy said.

"But it's just a scrap of paper," Pinocchio said. "What sort of a gift is that?"

Jiminy smiled. "You might be surprised."

Geppetto took a break from his work to share a Christmas Eve dinner with his son. After the meal, Pinocchio gave Geppetto his gift.

"What's this?" he asked.

"Your Christmas present," Pinocchio replied. "I hope you like it."

Geppetto untied the bow and tore the wrapping paper away.

"Why… this is the perfect present!" he exclaimed. "I could use an extra pair of hands in my workshop. How did you know, Pinocchio?"

Pinocchio just smiled. Jiminy had been right – he was surprised at how much joy his gift brought to his father.

"I'm glad to help," Pinocchio said. "I can start right now if you want."

Pinocchio cleared away the dinner dishes from the table, washed them and put them away. Then, he went to Geppetto's workshop. He swept up the wood shavings and boxed and wrapped the new toys. He made labels for each box so that Geppetto would know who each gift was for.

When Geppetto set out to deliver the last of the gifts, Pinocchio went up to bed. He was tired after helping his father all night. He was very pleased that he had made his father so happy. As he drifted off to sleep, he promised himself that he would help out more often.

That night, the Blue Fairy appeared.

"Because you have been so thoughtful this year, I have come to grant you one very special Christmas wish," she said. "Think carefully about what you want."

Pinocchio thought about the many things that he could ask for. But he still only wanted one thing.

"I want to give Geppetto the perfect Christmas gift," he told the Blue Fairy. "Something that he will love forever."

The Blue Fairy smiled. She knew just what the perfect present would be. "You are a very kind and loving boy, Pinocchio," she said. "I'm sure Geppetto will treasure this gift for years to come."

The next morning, Geppetto woke up early. He quietly went downstairs to light the fire and make breakfast. He was so happy that Pinocchio had helped him the night before, that he wanted to surprise his son. He wanted Pinocchio's first Christmas to be special.

Geppetto went to place his gifts for Pinocchio under the tree. He had carved a beautiful toy rocking horse and had crafted a playful jack-in-the-box. When he looked at the tree, he paused. Then, he gasped.

A puppet that looked exactly like his son hung from the branches.

"My dear Pinocchio!" Geppetto said with a smile.

He examined the puppet. It looked just like a puppet he had made a long time ago. One lonely night, he had made a wish on the Wishing Star that the puppet would turn into a real boy. The Blue Fairy had granted his wish and that was when Pinocchio the puppet had become his son.

When Pinocchio heard his father, he and Jiminy ran downstairs. "Merry Christmas," he shouted.

Geppetto sat in his favourite chair, holding the puppet. "My gift! How did you make it?"

Pinocchio stared at the copy of the puppet he used to be. He smiled. The Blue Fairy had chosen the perfect present for his father.

"Puppet Pinocchio was my favourite creation," Geppetto said. "Oh, how I've missed him."

A frown appeared on Pinocchio's face. "You have?" he asked. "Have I disappointed you?"

Geppetto laughed. "Not at all, son. You've been perfect in every way. This toy reminds me of how very much I wanted a real son. He reminds me of how happy I am to have you."

Pinocchio smiled. He went over to the puppet and looked at it closely. He felt as if he was looking into a mirror – the puppet had the same dark hair and blue eyes that he did.

Geppetto stood up and started dancing with the puppet and singing. Pinocchio clapped along. He was thrilled that his father was so happy.

Stopping to catch his breath, Geppetto looked at his son and said, "No one has ever thought to give me a toy of my own to play with because I'm a toy maker. You understand how much I love toys, Pinocchio. Thank you, son."

"See," Jiminy whispered to Pinocchio, "I told you that you would be surprised and now you've been surprised twice!"

Pinocchio nodded as he watched his father dance with the puppet some more. Then, he went over and danced beside the puppet that looked so much like him.

Geppetto held out the strings for Pinocchio so that he could try to make the puppet dance for himself. It was difficult, because the puppet was the same size as Pinocchio, but he didn't care. He was happy to share this moment with his father.

A little later, Pinocchio opened the gifts that Geppetto had placed under the tree for him. He laughed as the jack-in-the-box popped up and he rocked the small wooden horse across the floor. However, the best present that he'd received had come from the Blue Fairy. He would never forget the smile on his father's face. He hoped that they would share many more holidays just like this one.

Lady and the TRAMP
Lady's Christmas Surprise

It was the week before Christmas. Tramp and the puppies gathered beneath Jim and Darling's brightly decorated tree.

"You all know what holiday is coming up, right?" Tramp asked, his eyes twinkling.

"Of course, Dad," Scamp said. He was excited. Christmas was the puppies' favourite holiday. Lots of guests stopped by to wish Jim and Darling a happy holiday.

However, the best part of Christmas was the presents. The puppies got to help choose a special gift for each of their parents. They loved being trusted with two such important surprises.

"Do any of you kids know what your mother would like for Christmas?" Tramp asked.

"How about a steak from Tony's Restaurant?" Annette said.

Tramp shook his head. "We can do better than that."

"We need to give her something special," said Colette, "to show her how much we love her."

"Why don't you ask her what she'd like?" said Scamp, his voice muffled. He was chewing on a bow.

"We want to surprise her," Tramp reminded his son. He nudged him away from the presents. "That's the fun of Christmas."

"Maybe we'll find something on our walk today," Annette said.

Tramp thought that was a good idea. While Lady was taking a nap, he took the kids into town to look for the perfect present.

The village bustled with shoppers, their carriage wheels carving deep ruts in the snowy road.

The dogs rambled up and down the avenue, looking in all the shop windows. They saw sweaters, cushions, brush and comb sets, bowls and collars. But Tramp knew that none of these things were the perfect gift for Lady. He wanted to find her something special. Something that she would enjoy and that no other dog would have.

Tramp and the puppies kept looking into the store windows and they peeked at the packages that all the people were carrying. All they needed was one really good idea.

When the Sun started to sink in the sky, Tramp turned to the puppies and said, "We'd better head for the alleys and dig something from the trash."

As they crossed the road, Tramp noticed something sparkling in the snow. It was much brighter than an icicle. He turned it over with his paw.

"Holy hambones!" he cried. It was a gold and diamond necklace!

"What a bunch of rocks!" exclaimed Scamp.

"What a good stroke of luck!" remarked Annette.

"Just the right size for Mother!" added Colette.

Tramp smiled and then scooped up the necklace with his mouth. They'd found the perfect gift. He knew it would look beautiful on Lady.

Suddenly, Tramp dropped the necklace into the snow. It sparkled in the icy crystals. He frowned.

"What's the matter?" Scamp asked.

"This isn't right," Tramp muttered. Then he looked at his children. "Sorry, kids, but we have to return the necklace. It's not ours to take."

"But where would we go to return it?" Colette asked.

"Yeah, it was just here in the snow," Annette said. "How would we even find the owner?"

"I say finders keepers!" Scamp cried.

"Come on now, kids," Tramp said. "We can take it to the police. They'll know who to return it to."

With the puppies following, he bounded down the street to the station.

Inside, officers hurried around taking phone calls and writing reports.

"Stay close, kids," Tramp whispered to the puppies. "I don't want to lose you in the crowd."

Tramp trotted up to the front desk, with the puppies following behind. He dropped the necklace in front of the policeman in charge.

"What's this?" the officer said as he looked at the dog and then back to the necklace on the desk. He picked up the necklace and looked at the sparkling jewels.

Tramp panted and wagged his tail. The puppies stood eagerly beside him. Yip! Yip!

"You found it?" the officer asked.

Tramp nodded.

"Good dog!" he exclaimed.

The policeman took the necklace and began filling out his report while Tramp and the puppies watched.

At that moment, a woman rushed into the station. "Help!" she cried. "My necklace is gone! I'm offering a reward for its return."

The policeman smiled at the woman. Then, he held out the necklace. "Is this yours?" he asked. He pointed to Tramp. "This dog found it on the street and brought it here."

The woman gasped. "Thank you," she said. She scratched Tramp behind his ear. "How can I repay you?"

Woof! Tramp looked at the necklace.

"A new collar," she said. "That's it!"

She took Tramp and the puppies to the shop next door. Tramp walked up to the counter and picked up a gold collar with green stones that looked just like the woman's necklace.

"I'll take that one," the woman told the shopkeeper.

On Christmas morning Lady tore open the gift.

"You shouldn't have!" Her eyes sparkled like the green stones.

When Darling fastened the collar around Lady's neck, she pranced around the room as if she were a show dog.

"I love my new collar," Lady said. "What a wonderful Christmas surprise! But I love my family even more." She nuzzled Tramp and each of the puppies.

"Merry Christmas, Mother," said the puppies.

And it was a very merry Christmas, indeed.

Bambi

The Wonderful Winter Tree

Bambi awoke one morning to find that the whole world was covered in a soft white blanket.

"What is it, Mother?" Bambi asked as he gazed around in wonder.

"This is snow," replied his mother. "It means winter is upon us."

"Snow!" said Bambi. He took a cautious step… and then another

… and another. He felt the icy crystals crunch underneath his hooves. He looked back at the tiny tracks he had made.

"I like snow!" Bambi said.

"Snow is pretty to look at," his mother told him, "but it makes winter hard for all the animals."

Bambi was about to ask her why winter was harder than other seasons, but just then, his friend Thumper came hopping over.

"Hiya, Bambi!" said the bunny. "Come on! Let's go sliding!" He led Bambi to the pond, which was frozen solid.

Thumper slapped at the ice with his foot. "Come on! It's all right," he told Bambi. "See! The water's stiff!"

Bambi saw his friend, Flower the skunk.

"You want to come sliding?" Bambi called, running over. "Thumper says the water's stiff."

Flower shook his head. "No thanks. I'm off to my den. I'm going to sleep through the winter." He yawned. "Goodbye, Bambi," he said.

"'Bye, Flower," said Bambi. Then he spied another friend, a squirrel, scurrying up an oak tree.

"The pond is stiff, Squirrel," called Bambi. "Want to come sliding with me?"

"Thanks," replied the squirrel as he ducked into a hollow in the tree, "but I have to store nuts for the long winter." He showed Bambi the pile he had already collected. "No sliding for me today."

So, Bambi headed back to Thumper and the ice-covered pond by himself.

By that time, Thumper was sliding across the ice with some of his sisters. They made it look so easy, but when Bambi stepped on the ice, he lost his balance straight away. His hooves went sliding in four different directions!

"Kind of wobbly, aren't ya," said Thumper. He laughed. "Come on, Bambi. You can do it!"

Bambi wasn't so sure. It seemed that sliding across the stiff water wasn't quite as much fun for deer as it was for rabbits. And it also made him hungry. He said goodbye to the bunnies and went back to find his mother.

"Mother, I'm hungry," Bambi told her.

In the spring, summer and autumn, they had been able to find food almost anywhere they looked. Now that it was winter, Bambi could see that finding food wasn't so easy. There were no leaves on the trees and the grass was covered with snow and ice. The snow was so cold that when he poked through it, Bambi thought his nose might freeze.

At last, Bambi's mother uncovered a small patch of grass and Bambi nibbled it eagerly.

55

Then, Bambi curled up with his mother for a nap. The ground was hard and cold, and the wind was chilly. Bambi was grateful to have his mother there to keep him warm.

"Is this why the birds fly south and why our other friends sleep through the winter?" Bambi asked her.

His mother nodded and snuggled even closer. "But don't worry, Bambi," she told him. "Winter doesn't last forever."

By the end of December, there seemed nothing left in the forest for Bambi to eat but bitter bark. The days grew short and the nights grew long, and throughout them, Bambi's stomach rumbled. Then one day, something truly amazing happened.

Thumper was the first to see it. "Hey, Bambi!" he shouted. "Would you look at that tree!"

Bambi followed Thumper's paw. He could not believe his eyes.

57

There before them was a tall pine tree unlike any Bambi had ever seen. It was draped with strings of bright berries and yummy popcorn, and from the end of each branch hung a ripe, juicy apple. Bambi thought that the most wonderful thing was the gold star at the very top.

"Mother!" exclaimed Bambi. "Look what Thumper found!"

Slowly and cautiously, his mother drew closer. "It can't be…." she whispered. "It seems almost too good to be true."

"What is it, Mother?" Bambi asked her.

"The most beautiful tree in the world," she answered. She smiled down at Bambi. "What a special gift to have on your first Christmas."

"Who left it, Mother?" Bambi asked.

"I don't know," she replied.

"Maybe someone who loves animals," Thumper said, hopping up and down. "This is the best gift ever." He sniffed one of the apples hanging low to the ground.

"Can we share this food with every one of our friends, Mother?" Bambi asked.

"Yeah, and with my sisters, too?" Thumper chimed in.

"I don't see why not," Bambi's mother said. "Christmas is a time to share what we have with those we love."

Bambi and Thumper danced happily around the tree.

"Look at all the popcorn and berries!" Thumper cried. "And look at that star at the tippy-top, too!"

Bambi stopped prancing. He looked up at the golden star at the top of the tree. Then he looked up at the sky above him. The Sun was just beginning to go down. He knew that very soon, there would be a star twinkling in the sky just like the one at the top of the tree. A gentle hush fell over the clearing.

He danced back over to his mother and took a big bite out of one of the juicy green apples. Mmm! he thought. Nothing had ever tasted so good!

Gazing up at the star and at the wonderful winter tree, Bambi could feel a happy, warm glow swelling inside him. There was enough food on the tree to feed all the animals who were hungry. What a magical gift, thought Bambi. Winter was long and hard… and yet wonderful, after all.

DUMBO

The Best Christmas

One December morning, Dumbo the flying elephant woke up to find the circus grounds strangely quiet. He stuck his head outside his tent. Where was everyone?

Then Timothy Mouse appeared. "It's the Christmas holiday," he announced. "Time to sleep late, play in the snow and get ready for the holidays!"

Dumbo looked puzzled.

"Aw, don't tell me you've never heard of Christmas before," Timothy said in disbelief.

"Hey, fellas," he called up to the crows, "come on down here. I need help explaining Christmas to Dumbo."

The birds gathered around the elephant and began to chatter all at once.

"Why, Christmas is packages wrapped up in shiny paper."

"Now wait a minute! What about fancy holiday food?"

"Don't forget a big tree covered in ornaments and lights."

"And music! You can't have Christmas without carols!"

"Now do you understand?" Timothy asked Dumbo.

The elephant shook his head. He was even more confused.

"Hmmm," Timothy said, "this is gonna be harder than I thought." He and the crows huddled together and quickly came up with a new plan.

"Dumbo," said Timothy, "forget telling you about Christmas, we're gonna show you!"

Timothy Mouse scampered up onto Dumbo's cap. "Get ready for take-off!" he cried.

The crows took to the sky. Dumbo flapped his ears and followed right behind them. They flew and flew until, finally, a magnificent skyline came into view.

"Welcome to New York City!" Timothy announced. "I can't think of a more Christmassy place – except maybe the North Pole!" Timothy had grown up in New York and he thought it was the best place on Earth.

The little mouse gave Dumbo a tour of the bustling city. He showed the elephant the most festive place in New York first.

"That's Rockefeller Center," Timothy pointed out as they flew over a large tree.

Below, ice skaters glided and twirled around a sparkling outdoor rink. Dumbo couldn't take his eyes off the enormous tree, covered from top to bottom in twinkling lights and pretty decorations.

Timothy could tell that Dumbo was impressed. "What did I tell you?" the mouse asked. "People here don't just deck the halls – they decorate everything!"

Dumbo looked at all the people on the streets, full of holiday cheer. Some carried brightly wrapped packages. Some were singing carols. Everyone was in awe of the great big tree.

The sights and sounds of Christmas made Dumbo feel very happy. He couldn't wait to find out more about the holiday!

Timothy Mouse and Dumbo flew down Fifth Avenue, where the shop windows were filled with beautiful Christmas displays. Dumbo watched the shoppers hurrying around with large bags of presents.

Timothy saw something else.

"Hmm, that's strange," he said.

"People keep leaving presents in a box in front of that store over there. Come on, let's go and find out what's going on."

When Dumbo swooped down closer to the crowd, everyone cheered. They had never seen a flying elephant before. Dumbo felt like he was performing in one of his shows.

"What are the presents for?" Timothy Mouse asked a woman. "Is it the store's birthday or something?"

The woman chuckled. Then she explained that the packages were toys for children.

"There's just one problem," she continued. "The snow has slowed down traffic and I don't know how we're going to make all our deliveries on time. The boys and girls will be so disappointed if they don't get their presents this year!"

Timothy looked at Dumbo. Dumbo looked at Timothy. "Are you thinking what I'm thinking?" the mouse asked.

Dumbo nodded enthusiastically.

"Lady," said Timothy, "Dumbo and I would be happy to help spread a little Christmas cheer. I know this city like the back of my hand and Dumbo here never needs to worry about stuff like traffic. You can consider those presents as good as delivered!"

The people on the sidewalk cheered. "Thank you, Dumbo," one man said. "I knew Santa had flying reindeer, but I didn't know he had a flying elephant!"

"Shhh," Timothy replied with a mischievous wink. "It's supposed to be a secret!"

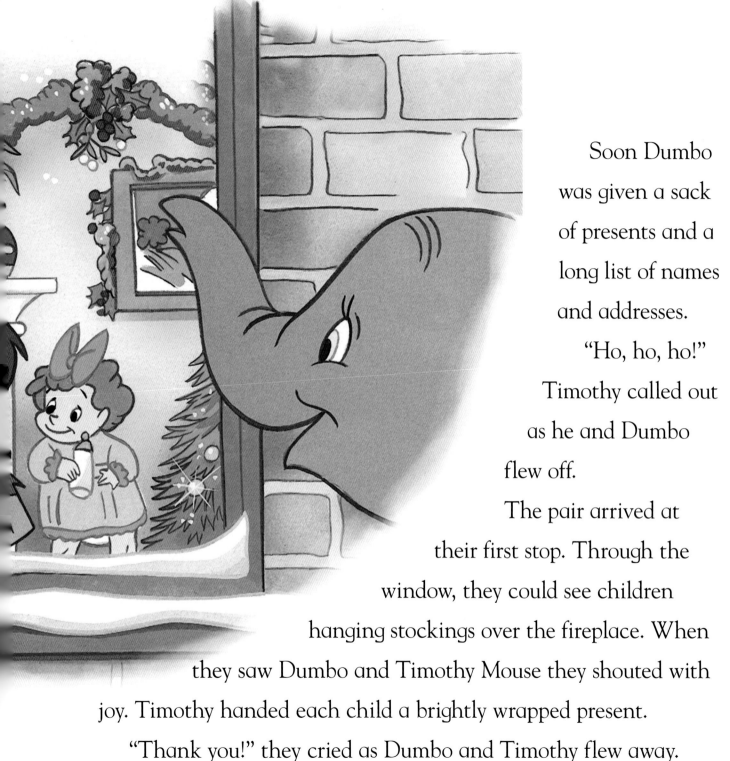

Soon Dumbo was given a sack of presents and a long list of names and addresses.

"Ho, ho, ho!" Timothy called out as he and Dumbo flew off.

The pair arrived at their first stop. Through the window, they could see children hanging stockings over the fireplace. When they saw Dumbo and Timothy Mouse they shouted with joy. Timothy handed each child a brightly wrapped present.

"Thank you!" they cried as Dumbo and Timothy flew away. "And Merry Christmas!"

Dumbo and Timothy flew from one house to another. They dropped off dolls and dump trucks, books and building blocks, puppets and puzzles. Every once in a while, the crows took a break from sightseeing to pitch in and sing some Christmas music. They were the funniest carol singers that the kids had ever seen!

Timothy's favourite part was watching the children and their parents when they spied Dumbo outside their windows. They'd blink and rub their eyes, wondering if what they were seeing could possibly be real.

"What's the matter?" Timothy would say playfully. "Haven't you ever seen a flying elephant before?" Then he'd laugh.

Dumbo loved the way that the children's faces lit up when he gave them their presents. It made him feel happy right down to his toes.

"We'll come back to visit them again soon, Dumbo," said Timothy as they headed home. "I promise."

Back at the circus grounds, Timothy and Dumbo settled down for the night.

"So, Dumbo," Timothy asked, "now do you know what Christmas is all about?"

Dumbo wasn't listening, though. He was thinking of all the children he had met that day and how he and Timothy had made them all smile. It had been the best Christmas.

Seeing Dumbo's happy expression, Timothy said, "Yup, I think you do."

The two tired friends soon fell fast asleep. That night, for the first time ever, Dumbo's dreams – and his heart – were filled with the magic of Christmas.

Disney • PIXAR

WALL•E

A Gift for WALL•E

WALL·E and EVE peeked over the top of a pile of garbage. The humans were acting very strangely. What were they up to now?

They saw two men stringing small coloured lights along a rusty iron fence. Another set up a plastic statue of a fat, white-bearded man in a red suit, red hat and black boots. A woman propped up a fake silver tree and decorated it with shiny red and green glass balls. Now that people had returned to live on Earth along with robots, they were always doing something that surprised WALL·E and EVE, but even for humans, they were acting very strangely.

Weirdest of all, the Captain from the *Axiom* was singing in a loud, joyful voice!

WALL·E and EVE listened to the words carefully. Confused, they looked at each other. Rudolph? A glowing nose? They thought Rudolph must be a kind of robot, like WALL·E and EVE. Neither of them had ever heard of a reindeer-bot before!

WALL·E and EVE snuck closer to where the humans were working. They called their bot friends over. While all the robots watched curiously, the humans hung a green circle with small red dots on a storefront. More of the humans started singing. One small girl even shook a silver ball.

Some of the robots had seen behaviour like this before, when they were living on the spaceship, *Axiom*. It usually happened every twelve months. They had never been able to figure it out.

WALL·E looked closely at the humans. He tried to figure out what made this so different. Then he put his little metal finger on it – the humans looked happy! Most of the time on the *Axiom* they had looked tired and bored, but there was something about what they were doing right now, here on Earth, that made them all very happy.

If it made the humans so happy, WALL·E thought then maybe it would make the robots happy, too!

For hours, the robots studied the humans. They stored what they had seen in their computer brains. Then, they set out to copy the humans.

Some of the bots picked up trash that the humans had used: bits of tinsel, fake holly, and scraps of brightly coloured paper.

The light bots collected hundreds of strings of lights. WALL·E already had a couple in his trailer. He'd always thought they were pretty and EVE loved them.

The bots draped WALL·E's trailer with lights. When the electricity was turned on, the lights shined so brightly they looked like a supernova.

M-O hung up old socks on the other wall. He had no idea why anyone would want to put socks on the wall, but if the humans were doing it, so would he!

The vacuum bot sucked up boxes and boxes of packing peanuts. Unfortunately, he also vacuumed up a nose full of dust.

"Ahhhh-chOOOO!" he sneezed. Little white peanuts floated down from the air, coating the floor with a blanket of snow.

WALL·E and EVE roamed around the grounds outside the trailer looking for more things to use. WALL·E went one way. EVE went the other.

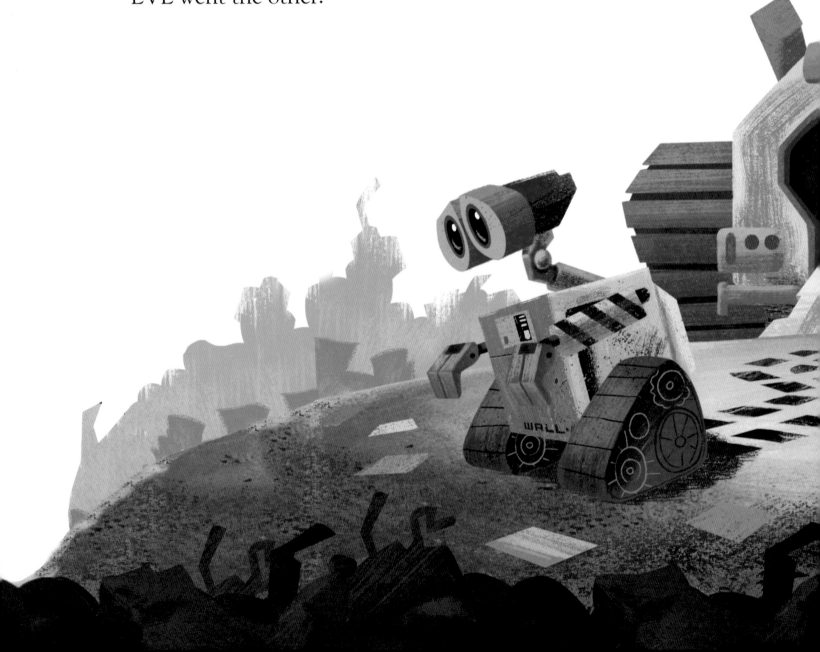

EVE picked up a piece of shiny metal. She found some scraps of wrapping paper. She stored them inside her chest cavity.

Suddenly, she heard two humans talking. One of them was the Captain.

"I just love Christmas, don't you?" the other human said. "The lights, the decorations, the sweets, the presents. Christmas is my favourite time of year!"

Christmas! What a lovely word! EVE rolled it around in her mind. It sparked all her circuits. Was this the name for what the humans were doing?

She stopped to listen more closely to what they were saying.

"Yes," said the Captain slowly. "But don't forget, Christmas isn't about things. That's just what Buy-n-Large wants us to believe. It's about *giving*, not just *getting* presents. It's about showing your friends and family that you care."

The Captain's words hummed inside EVE. Robots didn't have family, but they did have friends. She had one friend in particular, who meant more to her than any other – WALL·E. He had come to save her when she was on the ship. He had given her his spare parts. He had cared for her and watched over her. She needed to show him that she appreciated him.

But what kind of a present would do that?

EVE roamed far and wide. She searched and searched. She found many pieces of junk. None of them were quite right. Then, far away from WALL·E's trailer, her gaze locked on the perfect present.

Two days later, it was Christmas Eve. The bots had prepared a human-like celebration. Some of the smaller bots were stirring with excitement. The umbrella bot wore a pointy red hat with a white pom-pom on top.

The robots beeped out the words to the songs they had heard. They didn't always understand the human words so they made up some of their own.

While all the bots were celebrating the holiday in their own high-tech way, EVE pulled WALL·E aside. She held out a present wrapped in a pretty patterned paper.

WALL·E looked surprised. "Ee-vah?" he asked.

EVE nodded.

WALL·E turned the present this way and that. He admired how the shiny paper shimmered in the coloured lights. He was so busy looking at the present that he almost missed EVE motioning to him.

Open it, EVE signalled.

WALL·E carefully unwrapped the present. He folded up each scrap of paper and laid it on the ground next to him. Finally, he pulled away the last piece.

WALL·E held a little evergreen tree in his hands – a miniature Christmas tree.

The longer version of EVE's name was Extra-terrestrial Vegetation Evaluator. She had been trained to find plants and was drawn to this little tree. She knew that WALL·E, with his kind ways and big heart, would take care of this present, this living thing, better than anyone.

WALL·E and EVE went outside. Together they dug a hole in the earth and planted the Christmas tree. WALL·E placed a shiny silver star on the top.

WALL·E and EVE looked at the tree. The star twinkled brightly. It reflected the light from the real stars shining in the night sky, far above.

EVE reached out her hand. WALL·E took it. "Ee-vah," he said. Now he understood why humans liked Christmas so much.

Disney·PIXAR
MONSTERS, INC.
Christmas Laughs

Mike Wazowski, the green one-eyed monster, was on the Monsters, Inc. Laugh Floor. He couldn't keep from looking at the Laugh Meter. It showed all of the laughs that the monsters had collected by telling kids jokes. The laughs were turned into energy for the city of Monstropolis.

Monsters, Inc. had always been able to collect enough laughs to make sure that the monsters never had to worry about losing power. However, with Christmas around the corner, it seemed as if more and more kids were on holiday. That made it harder to collect laughs.

Mike was worried that there wouldn't be enough power to light up the Christmas tree in the city centre. Everybody looked forward to this Monstropolis tradition!

"Come on, monsters," he called out. "Think funny!"

Mike watched one monster go through a child's wardrobe door. When he came back onto the Laugh Floor, Mike looked at the canister that collected laughs. It wasn't even half full.

Just then, Sulley showed up. The big, furry blue monster
was the president of Monsters, Inc. He was also Mike's best friend.

"How's it going, Mike?" asked Sulley.

"Fine, fine," Mike answered nervously. He didn't want his boss
to know that they were running short on laughs. "That
Christmas tree will be lit up in no time."

Mike saw Sulley peek over at the Laugh
Meter. "I bet there are a lot of kids who
are—" Sulley started.

"No time to talk, buddy," Mike
cut him off. He guided Sulley
towards the door. "Got to get back
to work and collect those laughs."

"Okay," said Sulley. "See
you later."

As soon as Sulley left, Mike called out again, "Let's go, let's go! Collect those laughs! Christmas is just around the corner!"

The monsters worked even harder at being funny and entertaining. One monster even juggled seven plates and spun another plate on his head. The kid watching him broke into giggles and clapped wildly. The laugh canister quickly filled up.

George, a big, furry orange monster went through another child's door. He sat on a stool next to the little girl's bed, holding a microphone in one hand.

"Hey, is this thing on? Hello?" George said, tapping the microphone. "Ready to have some laughs? Good. Why did the monster eat a lightbulb?"

"Why?" the child asked.

"He needed a light snack!" George exclaimed, and the little girl roared with laughter. "Wait, wait! I have more." He told another joke that sent the child into giggles. On the Laugh Floor, Mike watched the canister outside the door fill up.

"Nice work," Mike said when George had finished.

"Thanks," George said. He and Mike looked up at the Laugh Meter on the wall. It was growing steadily, much to everyone's delight.

"We actually might make our goal," Mike said with a hopeful smile.

All of a sudden, Mike and the other monsters watched in horror as the Laugh Meter began to go down instead of up!

"What's going on? What's happening?" Mike said, his voice growing louder.

The laugh wranglers, Smitty and Needleman, weren't sure.

"This has never happened before," said Smitty, the head wrangler.

"Well, don't just stand there," Mike cried. "Fix it!"

The wranglers sprang into action. After a while, they discovered a leak in the laugh tank, where all the laughs were stored.

The monsters on the Laugh Floor were worried. They wondered if all of their hard work had been for nothing.

"Ho, ho, ho!" came a cheerful voice.

Mike looked up and saw Santa Claus walking onto the floor. Then he realized that it was Sulley dressed in a Santa suit.

"I'm just getting into the Christmas spirit," Sulley explained. Then he looked around. "It looks like I'm the only one. What's going on?"

Mike explained the problem. "But I've got everything under control, Santa, er, Sulley."

"I'm sure you do," Sulley replied. "I'm just going to see if there's anything I can do to help."

Sulley followed Mike into the basement of Monsters, Inc., where the laugh wranglers were hard at work. Everyone wanted to get the laugh tank fixed as soon as possible and time was running out. The tree-lighting ceremony was only a few hours away!

The wranglers couldn't agree on how to fix the problem.

"Anything I can do?" Sulley asked.

"One of the pipes that leads into the laugh tank has burst," explained Smitty. "We need to tie it off, but none of our tools are strong enough to turn the pipe."

Hmm… said Sulley, scratching his head.

Then, Mike had a great idea. "Why not actually tie it off?" Since Sulley was so strong, he could bend that pipe right into a pretzel shape!

Sulley was willing to give it a try. Mike stood by his side and coached him.

It worked! The pipe stopped leaking!

Mike and Sulley headed back up to the Laugh Floor. All the monsters congratulated Sulley!

Mike wondered why no one was thanking him. It had been his idea, after all! But there was no time to think about that now.

"We're back up and running!" Mike announced. "Let's make some laughs!"

All the monsters got to work. They knew they'd have to work extra hard to make up for all the lost laughs.

Sulley decided to jump in and help. "Hey, we've only got a couple of hours to get the tree lit," he said to Mike.

Still dressed as Santa, Sulley went through a child's wardrobe door.

When he came back onto the Laugh Floor, he looked up at the Laugh Meter on the wall. It was increasing, but slowly.

"We've got to make it," Sulley whispered to Mike.

Finally, the Laugh Meter was back up to the level it had been before the leak. Sulley looked at the clock on the wall and frowned. It was only thirty minutes until the tree-lighting ceremony.

Suddenly, Sulley had an idea. "The only way we're going to make our laugh quota is to get some really over-the-top laughs."

Mike nodded in agreement.

"We need a grand slam here," continued Sulley. "We need a special kind of monster. One with perfect timing… star quality… a natural at comedy… a one-eyed sensation."

Mike realized what Sulley was trying to do. He crossed his arms and shook his head. "No, Sulley. Absolutely not."

"The Christmas tree lighting is only half an hour away," Sulley told him. "Come on, Mike. The whole city is depending on you."

That was all Mike needed to hear. "You're right. Let's do it!" he said. "But you're coming with me!"

Sulley and Mike went through a door together. Sulley was still dressed as Santa and Mike had dressed up as an elf. To their delight, a little girls' sleepover was going on!

Mike started with some of his best jokes. "Hey, Sulley, I've got to walk twenty-five miles to get home."

"Why don't you take a train?" Sulley asked, playing along.

"I did once, but my mother made me give it back!" Mike said.

The kids in the room laughed, but not as hard as the monsters had hoped. After a few more jokes, Mike realized he'd have to try something else. He picked up the sack of toys that Sulley had brought in, but it was far too heavy for him.

"Whoa!!" he exclaimed as he tripped. He landed upside down and the sack of toys spilled out around him. He sat up with a doll draped over his head and a toy race car stuck to his foot.

The kids roared with laughter. They begged for more and Mike happily tumbled and tripped for them again.

Mike and Sulley made it back onto the Laugh Floor in time to watch the Laugh Meter hit its limit!

At the tree-lighting ceremony, Mike and Sulley stood proudly in the front of the crowd.

Sulley leant over and whispered in Mike's ear, "You did a great job. Thank you."

Mike smiled. "You know what I always say: funny doesn't grow on trees. When you got it, you got it. And I got it."

Sulley laughed. He was happy Mike had it – and shared it. It was going to be a bright Christmas, after all.

Winnie the Pooh

The Sweetest Christmas

One snowy Christmas Eve, Winnie the Pooh looked up and down, in and out, and all around his house.

He had a tree set up in his living room. It was decorated with some candles in honey pots.

Pooh looked at the tree and tapped his head.

"Something seems to be missing," he said.

He walked over to the window and peered outside. Then, he walked back to the tree and thought some more.

Suddenly, a knocking sound startled Pooh. *Rap-a-tap-tap!* He turned towards his front door.

"Maybe whatever it is I can't remember I'm missing is outside my door," Pooh said.

When Pooh opened the door, he found a small snowman on his front step.

"H-h-he-l-l-l-o, P-Pooh B-Bear," the snowman said as he shivered.

Pooh thought the voice sounded very familiar. He invited the snowman inside.

After standing beside the fire for a few minutes, the snowman began to melt. The more he melted, the more he started to look like Piglet!

"Oh, my," said Pooh. He was happy to see his friend where there used to be a snowman.

"Oh, my," said Piglet. Now that the snow had melted off him, he could see Pooh's glowing Christmas tree.

"Are you going to string popcorn for your tree?" Piglet asked.

"There was popcorn and string," Pooh admitted. "But now there is only string."

Pooh thought some more, wondering if popcorn was what he'd forgotten. But that wasn't it, either.

"Then we can use the string to wrap the presents you're giving," Piglet said.

Something began to tickle at Pooh's brain. It was the something missing that he hadn't been able to remember.

"I forgot to get presents!" Pooh exclaimed.

"Don't worry, Pooh," Piglet said. "I'm sure you'll think of something."

Soon it was time for Piglet to go home and wrap his own presents. He said goodbye to his friend and went back out into the cold, snowy night.

Pooh stood beside his tree and tapped his head while he thought. Where could he find presents for his friends? It was already Christmas Eve. Was it too late?

He thought some more. He sat down in his cosy chair. Then he got up and had a small smackerel of honey. He peered out the window and watched the snow fall.

Then he had an idea.

He still didn't know what to do about the presents he'd forgotten, but he knew where to find help.

"Hello!" Pooh called as he knocked on Christopher Robin's door.

Christopher Robin opened the door and smiled when he saw the visitor.

"Come in, Pooh Bear," he said. "Merry Christmas! Why do you look so sad on the most wonderful night of the year?"

Pooh was just about to explain about the forgotten presents when something caught his eye. He pointed at the stockings over the fireplace. "What are those for?" he asked.

"Those are stockings to hold Christmas presents," explained Christopher Robin.

"But Christopher Robin," Pooh said, "what if someone forgot to find presents for his friends? And what if that same someone doesn't have stockings to hang because he doesn't wear any?"

Pooh looked down at his bare feet, then back up at Christopher Robin.

"Silly old bear," Christopher Robin said. He took Pooh up to his room. They dug through his drawers until Pooh found seven stockings.

"Thank you, Christopher Robin," Pooh said. He smiled. He'd picked a stocking for each of his friends to put their presents in: purple for Piglet, red-and-white striped for Tigger, orange for Rabbit, yellow for Eeyore, maroon for Gopher and blue for Owl. He also had one for him to hang over his fireplace.

He hurried off to deliver the stockings to his friends. As he walked through the Hundred-Acre Wood, he thought about the presents he still needed for the stockings.

"I will get the presents later," Pooh said to himself. "The stockings come first."

Pooh stopped at each of his friends' houses. Everyone was asleep. He quietly hung the stockings where his friends would find them. Each one had a tag that read: FROM POOH.

When Pooh got back to his house, he climbed into his cosy chair in front of a roaring fire.

"Now I must think about presents for my friends," he said.

Pooh was tired from finding the stockings and delivering them to his friends' houses. Before he knew it, his thinking turned into dreaming. He was fast asleep.

The next morning, Pooh awoke to a loud thumping noise. *Thump-a-bump-bump!*

"I wonder who that could be," he said. He climbed out of his chair and opened the door.

"Merry Christmas, Pooh!" his friends cried.

There on Pooh's doorstep stood Tigger, Rabbit, Piglet, Owl, Eeyore and Gopher. They were each carrying the stocking from Pooh.

Pooh scratched his head. All of a sudden he remembered what had happened the night before. He had fallen asleep before giving presents to his friends!

"Oh, bother," he said. Then he realized that his friends were all talking at once. They were thanking him for their gifts!

"No more cold ears in the winter with my new cap," Piglet said.

"My stripedy sleeping bag is tigger-ific!" exclaimed Tigger.

"So is my new carrot cover," Rabbit said.

"This rock-collecting bag will sure make work go faster," Gopher said.

Eeyore swished his tail to show Pooh his new tail-warmer. "No one's ever given me such a useful gift before," he said.

Owl told Pooh his new wind sock would help him with the day's weather report.

Pooh looked at his friends. They were very happy with their stockings, even though there weren't any presents in them!

"Something very nice is going on," Pooh said.

"It is very nice, Pooh Bear," Piglet said.

"It's called Christmas, buddy bear," Tigger said. He patted Pooh on the back.

Then, Pooh watched in surprise as each of his friends put a honey pot in his own stocking.

"I don't know what to say," Pooh told his friends. He was thrilled by their gifts. Honey was his favourite treat!

"Christmas is a wonderful holiday," Rabbit said. "Especially when you have good friends to share it with."

"Yep!" Tigger agreed. "But I know how we could make the day even sweeter."

He looked at the honey pot in Pooh's hands.

An idea tickled at Pooh's brain.

"Let's all have lunch together," Pooh said. He passed out the honey pots his friends had just brought him. "Christmas… what a sweet day, indeed."

101 DALMATIANS

The Puppies' First Christmas

One winter evening, Pongo and Perdita were watching TV with their puppies when a rustling noise in the hallway caught their attention. The puppies jumped off their chairs and ran to the doorway.

They all watched silently as Roger and Nanny hauled a huge tree into the parlour. It was fresh and green and made the room smell like a pine forest.

"What's going on?" Rolly asked, turning to look at his mother.

"Don't worry, dear," said Perdita. "It's Christmas Eve. This is just the beginning!"

"Chris-mess?" Lucky asked. "It does look like a mess." He wagged his tail.

The parlour floor was covered with pine needles, boxes of ornaments, tinsel garlands and strings of small lights.

Anita was waiting in the parlour to help Roger and Nanny. The puppies looked on in awe as their human pets began acting very strangely. Roger hung shiny coloured globes on the branches. Anita was winding a garland around the tree.

When the tree was finished and the room tidied, Roger flipped a switch. The lights and shiny ornaments cast a magical glow about the room. The puppies stared wide-eyed at the tree.

That night, when Pongo and Perdita tucked the puppies into their basket, they told them all about Christmas.

"It's a time when people show their families and friends how much they care for them," Pongo said. He explained how humans sent cards, baked cookies and fruitcakes and sang festive carols.

"It may sound strange, but you'll grow to love the holiday season," Perdita said. She nuzzled Patch, who let out a yawn.

"Especially the beef bones left over from dinner," Pongo added.

"Bones?" Patch said, perking up. His father smiled.

"And that's not all," Perdita continued. "On Christmas Eve, after everyone's in bed, people sneak presents under the tree."

"Presents?" all the puppies said at once.

"What kind of presents?" Patch asked. "Can you wish for them?"

"I'd wish for a new bed," Lucky said as he climbed into the basket that he shared with his brothers and sisters.

"Why do people put presents under the tree?" Pepper asked.

"Christmas is about giving," Pongo told the puppies. "People give presents to their friends and family to show how much they love them."

"I wonder if we will get any presents?" said Rolly.

"Maybe," Perdita replied. "Anita gave me a new collar last year."

"And I got a red ball," said Pongo.

"I hope someone loves us," said Penny.

"You are all loved, whether or not there are presents under the tree," Perdita said. "Now time for bed. Tomorrow is a big day."

On Christmas morning, the puppies woke at dawn. They crept into the parlour. Sure enough, there were piles of brightly wrapped packages under the tree.

"We are loved!" Freckles cried.

The puppies dived into the pile of presents. They tossed the packages around and ripped and tore at the coloured paper.

"Christmas is fun!" Rolly exclaimed as he shook some wrapping paper out of his mouth.

Lucky pulled open a box. "Perfume?" he said and wrinkled his nose.

Penny dragged a spotted necktie out of some tissue paper. "What do I need with more spots?"

Freckles held up a lace handkerchief. "What is this for?" he asked.

Just then, they heard Rogers' and Anita's voices in the hallway.

The puppies looked at each other in alarm.

"Let's get out of here!" Rolly said. The puppies scampered around the room, hiding behind the sofa, under the chairs and in the folds of the curtains.

The puppies trembled when they heard Roger's footsteps.
He stopped in the doorway. "What on Earth?" he said.
Anita walked up beside him. "Oh, dear!" she cried.

"Perdita, Pongo," Roger called out.
"Where are you?"

The puppies
heard the click of
their parents' claws
on the wooden floor as
they scurried towards
the parlour.

When they came
into the room, Pongo
said, "Woof!"

And Perdita
repeated, "Woof!"

The puppies looked at each other uncertainly. "We're in for it now," Lucky whispered.

Then they heard something very strange. Anita started to laugh.

Roger said, with a chuckle, "Looks like we had some help opening our gifts."

"Wasn't that kind of the puppies!" Nanny said, as she walked into the room and saw the mess of paper and ribbon.

"I wonder where they've gone off to," Roger said with a twinkle in his eye. "Here, pups!"

"There are still so many boxes to unwrap," Anita said, shaking her head. "I do wish they'd come and help."

The puppies looked around at each other in their hiding places. Then, one by one, they crept out from under the chairs and behind the sofa.

They gathered around the tree as Roger pulled more packages from under the branches. "Go for it, boys and girls!"

Yip! Yip! The puppies tore into the bright wrappings and the tangled ribbons. They crunched cardboard and rolled around in the crinkly papers. Patch hopped into an empty box to hide. When Lucky started to tear at the top of the box, Patch popped up with a playful, "Woof!"

Pongo and Perdita looked at each other. "Shall we join them?" whispered Pongo.

"This is their first Christmas," Perdita replied. "Let them have their fun."

When the puppies grew tired of rolling around in the wrapping paper, Anita brought out a large basket.

"Sorry we didn't have time to wrap these," she said. "But then…" She smiled. "… maybe you've done enough work for today."

She handed each puppy a squeaky toy.

From the bottom of the basket she pulled out two Christmas jumpers for Pongo and Perdita.

"Anita knitted them herself," said Roger with pride.

That evening, after Christmas dinner was over, the puppies were still full of energy. They weren't ready to go to bed.

"We like Christmas!" said Pepper.

"We like our toys!" said Rolly.

"We like tissue paper!" said Patch.

"But remember what we told you about Christmas?" Perdita asked. She nudged her children towards their basket. "It's a time for giving."

"It's also about forgiving," Pongo said gently. "You were lucky that Roger and Anita weren't upset that you unwrapped their presents."

The puppies' heads drooped a little.

"We're lucky we have two wonderful humans," Perdita said softly. "That is the best present we could ask for."

The puppies raised their eyes to their mother hopefully.

"We are loved," Penny said. She smiled.

"You are all, each and every one of you, loved," Perdita assured her children.

"And that's what Christmas is really all about," Pongo said as the puppies drifted off to sleep.

THE END

TERENCE CONRAN
easy

living

conran
OCTOPUS

To help you have an easy and enjoyable life:

for Sebastian, Jasper, Tom, Sophie and Ned; Sam, Max, Finbar, Felix and Coco; Max, Toby and Harriet –
I hope you (and everyone else) will read the text as well as look at the pictures.

Commissioning Editor: Denny Hemming

Managing Editor: Richard Atkinson

Copy Editor: Helen Ridge

Design: Helen Lewis

Picture Research: Claire Taylor

Special Photography: James Mitchell

Special Photography Art Direction: Robin Rout

Production: Julian Deeming

Contributing Editor: Elizabeth Wilhide

Project Consultant: Simon Willis

Extracts from *How Proust Can Change Your Life*
by Alain de Botton are reproduced by permission of
Macmillan, London and Pantheon Books, New York.

Extracts from the works of Elizabeth David are reproduced
by permission of her Estate.

Extracts from *The Wind in the Willows* by Kenneth
Grahame © The University Chest, Oxford, reproduced by
permission of Curtis Brown, London.

First published in Great Britain in 1999
by Conran Octopus Limited
37 Shelton Street
London WC2H 9HN
a part of Octopus Publishing Group

© Conran Octopus Limited 1999

All rights reserved. No part of this book may be
reproduced, stored in a retrieval system, or transmitted
in any form or by any means, electronic, electrostatic,
magnetic tape, mechanical, photocopying, recording
or otherwise, without the prior permission in writing of
the publisher.

A catalogue record for this book is available from the
British Library.

ISBN: 1 84091 002 X

Colour origination by Sang Choy International, Singapore
Printed in China

contents

introduction 6

elements 16

comfort 66

function 120

detail 176

introduction

Whenever I am approached to give advice on interior design, I have a sneaking suspicion that what I am expected to provide is an instant set of style rules – a tried and tested formula that could be applied in every circumstance, guaranteeing 'perfect' results every time – or, at the very least, a list of my favourite colours and products for others to follow like a blueprint.

Instead, I usually answer that the first thing people should do is to take all of their possessions and pile them up outside their front door. Then, they should look long and hard at the basic shell that remains. Once this framework is right – when the spaces, the lighting, the services, the structure, the surfaces and finishes have been sorted out – then, and only then, should they think about which of their belongings to bring back indoors, keeping only those things that contribute something positive to their lives, whether aesthetically, emotionally or practically.

Of course, I am not seriously suggesting that every front garden up and down the country should suddenly be transformed into a reject pile ready for the skip, dump or boot sale – but I am only half joking. The basic attitude lying behind this superficially impractical strategy is one that I firmly believe to be important.

Where we live must work from the inside out, and from the ground up. This means taking where we are and who we are as starting points, not applying a set of arbitrary criteria dreamed up by somebody else. Only then can a home be a perfect fit, as comfortable as a favourite piece of clothing.

As modern life becomes ever more complex and fast paced, our homes must increasingly act as antidotes to stress and tension, as places to relax, unwind and be ourselves: essentially, as spaces for easy living. This function is not new: ever since industrialization,

the home has been a refuge, a necessary counterpoint to the world of work. What has changed, however, is that the need for space, privacy and comfort has become much more acute.

Easy living, however, is not about sinking into a mindless stupor. Living in a cocoon is one answer to the complexities and hardships of everyday life but it is ultimately a defensive, if not a negative stance. Instead, by 'easy' I mean the physical ease of simplicity, where practical tasks can be performed without frustration, fuss or muddle, where upkeep is straightforward and there is enough space and light to go round. This is largely, although not exclusively, a matter of getting the basic framework right. But, at the same time, 'easy' also implies the psychological freedom of coming through the front door and experiencing the sensation of kicking off your shoes – even if only mentally. This happens when your home provides room for self-expression and pleasure, when it feels like yours and not anyone else's and when it enables you to stay in touch with what you enjoy.

When it comes to easy living, rules only confuse the picture. Bombarded with advice and baffled by the myriad choices of the consumer world, establishing what you want and like is not so much a learning process, but more of a relearning process. It's a question of recognition. Focusing on those simple pleasures that make life worth living yet rarely stand out as high points in your personal history is enough to provide the direction you need. Sounds, smells and other less tangible triggers help to unlock the memory bank and identify what makes you feel good. Many of these elements will inevitably be common pleasures shared by us all, though no less important for that. Others will be more particular, related to a specific experience or event that has a personal meaning.

Easy living means opening your eyes to the beauty of everyday things, natural or man-made.

Holiday experiences – walking
barefoot on the sand, smelling
the salt tang of cool sea breezes,
camping out in the wild – remind
us that pleasures can be simple.

Vita Sackville-West, in a talk broadcast on BBC radio in 1950, identified a whole range of insignificant, essentially domestic pleasures that everyone has experienced from time to time but hardly ever remarks upon. In the family shorthand, which gave the talk its title, these brief moments of satisfaction were collectively termed 'through leaves', after the 'small but intense pleasure of walking through dry leaves and kicking them up as you go'. It was 'through leaves' to run a stick along an iron railing or to crunch thin ice; to suddenly remember a word or name you thought you'd forgotten; or to write with the perfect pen nib. So was pulling curtains that ran freely on their rods, sliding out the drawer of a steel filing cabinet which opened 'readily and silkily' on ball bearings, cutting pages of a book with a sharp paper-cutter, or drawing a cork with a good patent corkscrew. Drinking when you're thirsty, feeling sand between your toes at the seaside, reading in bed – that 'perfect moment' that lasts only as long as you can stay awake – sinking into bouncy seats at the cinema . . . . She concluded her talk by suggesting that her listeners come up with their own list of pleasures to add to those she had overlooked or forgotten.

It's an amusing exercise and a revealing one, as it shows how we don't necessarily have to go far and wide for our pleasures, since they are often right under our noses. Literally so, in many cases. A smell can be one of the most evocative spurs to the memory, conjuring rooms, events, periods of time we'd imagined that we had long forgotten. The wholesome smell of baking bread, the rich aroma of fresh coffee, the perfume of roses or lilies have an almost universal appeal, so much so that retailers often strategically employ such scents to whet the appetites of their customers. For me, it is damp earth in the rain or a fuggy greenhouse, cigar smoke, clean linen dried in the sun or the waft of pungent thyme on hot, dry Mediterranean air that summon up that same sense of well-being.

Enjoyable experiences are not always divisible into strict categories of sensation. Like Vita Sackville-West's 'through leaves', they come parcelled as snapshots of pleasure, where touch, sound, smell and sight all strike the same emotional chord – like waking up to find it has snowed overnight, shopping in an outdoor market, putting on a freshly ironed shirt or suddenly catching sight of the sea. I recently came across a café in Australia that filled me with an immense feeling of contentment, yet did so through very simple means. There was a big square table with people sitting casually round it drinking coffee and reading papers and, in the centre of the table, a large bowl of nobbly

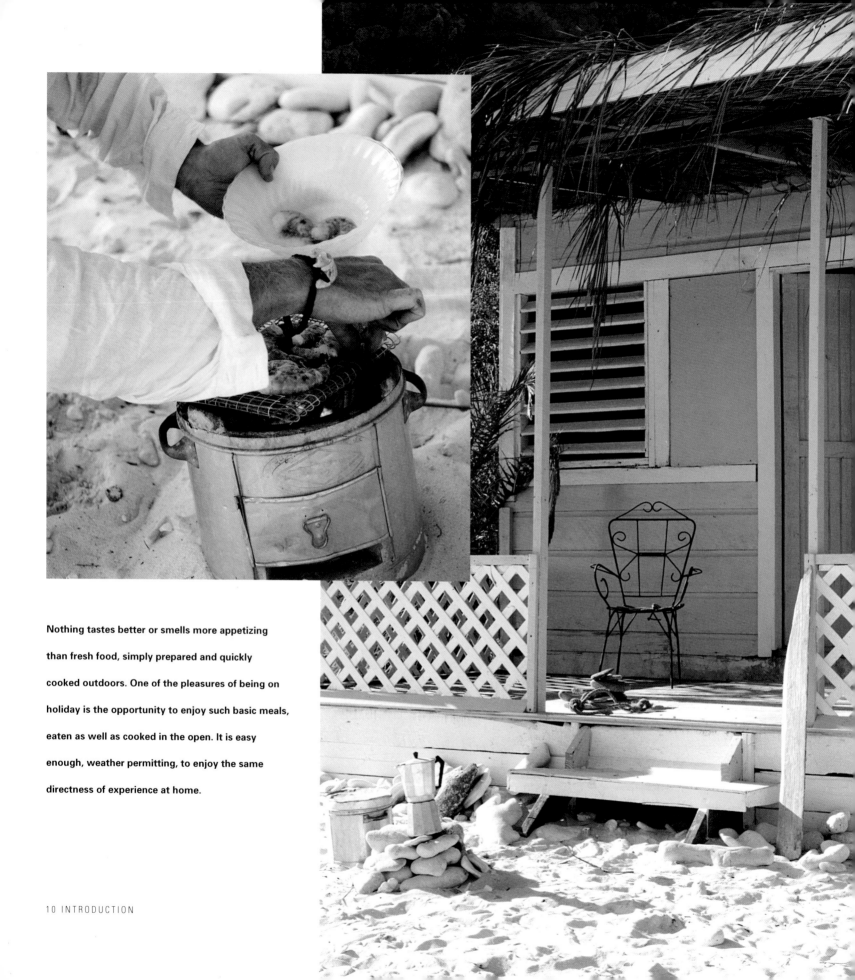

Nothing tastes better or smells more appetizing
than fresh food, simply prepared and quickly
cooked outdoors. One of the pleasures of being on
holiday is the opportunity to enjoy such basic meals,
eaten as well as cooked in the open. It is easy
enough, weather permitting, to enjoy the same
directness of experience at home.

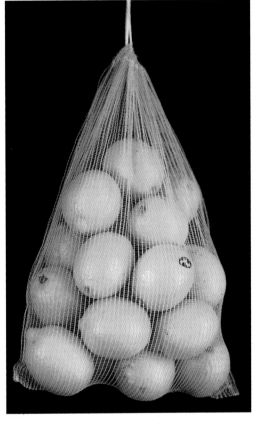

lemons, with their leaves still attached. Nothing could be more straightforward or more suggestive of conviviality. It was a place where you simply wanted to sit down and join in. In the same way, the sight of a long table set up outdoors and covered with a white cloth can convey a mood of hospitality and celebration before the food is even laid out, while a crackling log fire – sight, smell, sound and warmth all coming together in one focus – evokes an instant sense of security, comfort and nostalgia.

When you stop to consider, easy living is what most people want from a holiday. Once or twice a year, we invest money in the quest for fine weather, good food, beautiful surroundings and an escape from all that makes life complicated and demanding. Two weeks later we are back at home, where the holiday spirit often wears off as fast as the suntan. There is no reason why this should be so.

The strong light of southern latitudes adds a particular vibrancy to colours. The many evocative blues of the Mediterranean and the hotter, spicier shades of Asia and Latin America appear more intense and more saturated there than under grey, northern skies. Or perhaps it is just a question of taking the time to look: when you are in the right frame of mind, colour sings out of details, no matter how insignificant they may at first seem.

Compartmentalizing life, so that contact with simple pleasures must be fitted into a scheduled slot, is the essence of modern alienation. The best souvenir we can bring back from holiday is the will to make everyday life more in tune with what we really enjoy.

Good holidays do not necessarily depend on exotic locations and luxurious accommodation, pleasurable though these may be. Many people choose to take their breaks in considerably simpler circumstances than those in which they live at home. Camping out in basic cottages or villas beside the sea or in the mountains, with only those belongings that fit in a suitcase or rucksack, coping with rudimentary facilities, stocking up at local markets and quaysides and passing days at a time without the intrusion of newspapers, television or a ringing telephone can be heaven on earth. Lying in the sun, swimming in the sea, taking brisk walks in the fresh air or even a good downpour replace the daily grind of commuting in stuffy trains, brooding at a computer terminal or sitting motionless in traffic jams. For people who choose to take such holidays, economy is far from being the most persuasive factor.

Easy living is about providing the means to experience things directly, without the distancing intervention of technology or the burden of too many possessions. This is a salutary lesson in an age when machines are assumed to be the panacea for many ills, delivering convenience at the touch of a button, and when acquiring more and more material goods has become an aim in itself. Easy living on holiday, when we find that we can manage perfectly well without nine-tenths of what our home contains, helps to remind us that machines break down, need servicing and maintenance and that possessions clamour to be organized, stored and looked after. When too much is on offer, we are beset by a series of niggling choices that obscure real advantages of practicality and beauty.

Holidays also offer an essential breathing – and thinking – space. During a recent holiday, I read *How Proust Can Change Your Life* by Alain de Botton. He describes how Proust encouraged a discontented young man, frustrated by his dreams of palatial luxury, to look at the still-life paintings of Chardin. By studying the everyday objects depicted – 'bowls of fruit, jugs, coffee pots, loaves of bread,

On holiday, there is time to pay attention to more intangible elements, such as the quality of light. The grey, misty light of a northern seashore emphasizes the feeling of distance and the expansiveness of a sea view; while winter landscapes, with light reflected upwards from snow and ice, have a stark, graphic quality that accentuates form.

In steamy, tropical locations, outdoor living comes into its own. Owned by an American artist, this house in southern Sri Lanka (right), with its deep columned veranda and seating area among the palms, is perfectly in tune with its setting.

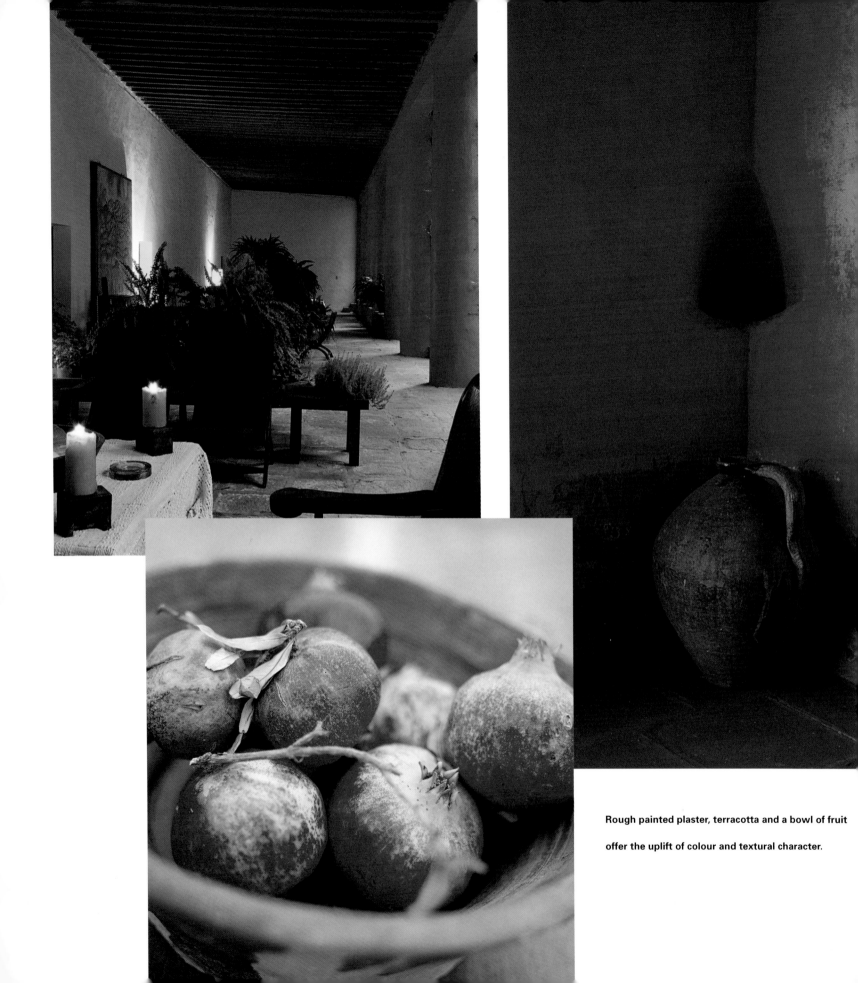

Rough painted plaster, terracotta and a bowl of fruit

offer the uplift of colour and textural character.

knives, glasses of wine, slabs of meat' – Proust believed the young man would realize he was already surrounded by beauty. In Chardin's paintings, such beauty was suggested in a 'harmony' between objects, for example, 'almost a friendship between the reddish colours of a hearthrug, a needle box and a skein of wool'. But it was also evident in the sensuality of visual experience that great painters can convey, such as 'the play of light on the end of the spoon, the fibrous softness of a tablecloth, the velvety skin of a peach'. Proust was demonstrating how happiness and contentment can come from learning a new way of looking at one's surroundings.

I cannot pretend, though, that easy living is necessarily doing it on the cheap. There is also a certain price to be paid in terms of work and time. Good materials that age well, thoughtful design and the finesse of detail tend to cost money and effort – but then, in the long run, so do shoddy products that break or wear out quickly and need to be replaced. And it can be just as expensive and laborious, if not more so, to repeatedly succumb to the marketable 'look' of the moment. The alternative – making choices by default, tinkering with problems rather than solving them, adopting second-best solutions because they are cheaper, haphazardly acquiring a collection of products and furnishings that say nothing and mean even less – often just results in a home that neither works very well nor feels right.

I have always felt that one of the greatest compliments a visitor to your home can pay you is to sit down and take off their jacket unprompted, to be as relaxed in your surroundings as you are. Yet how do you make it happen? To me, easy living in its widest sense is the natural by-product of good design. Although serendipity may come into it, it isn't completely accidental: on the contrary, comfort, simplicity, pleasure and practicality can come only from informed choice and creative application.

In the context of home design, choice has never been greater. But without a deeper understanding of why and how different elements work, choice can be meaningless. The design process itself can be seen as a series of choices, not, as is all too often supposed, choices based on looks alone, but a continual testing of parameters and weighing of alternatives. Beyond the superficialities of style are the essential qualities that make all the difference: the integrity of materials, the refinements of construction or manufacture, the inspiration of wit and imagination.

I believe that where and how we live is fundamental to our well-being; such considerations are too important to be sidelined into a holiday break and sidestepped the rest of the year. Things that work well, look beautiful, evoke memories and express our personalities restore quality to everyday living.

elements

The home is an emotional concept as much as a physical, serviced structure: bricks and mortar, plumbing and wiring, as well as comfort, security and well-being. Such states of mind, however, are not produced out of thin air. Providing the essential psychological context for enjoying everyday life is often a question of getting the physical framework in order. This means thinking about your home in a basic, elemental way. Space, light, colour, texture and material quality operate on many levels that go far beyond the practical.

We do not experience these elements in complete isolation. Space and light, light and air, colour and texture are intrinsically interwoven and connected. Nevertheless, each element has its own impact on the picture, which can be revealed dramatically in simple alterations that you make to your surroundings. Improving a lighting arrangement, for example, can transform a room from somewhere that makes you feel jaded or ill at ease for no readily identifiable reason into a place that is positively alive with vitality and warmth. Although the change may be accomplished on a physical level, with fittings, light sources and wiring, the effect is profoundly emotional.

Joseph Ettedgui, innovative retailer and fashion entrepreneur, believes that lighting and flooring are the two most important elements in the home and if these work, 'everything else will look wonderful'. Whenever he is creating a home, he always spends as much money as possible on good quality flooring, whether stone, wooden parquet or the softest carpet. 'The floor is one of the very first things you feel when you enter a place,' he says. 'Your feet actually feel quite a lot.'

Paying attention to basic elements can also mean making the effort to fix fundamental problems. Sometimes it is difficult enough to identify the problems in the first place. Here, time is both an ally and an enemy. We are all familiar with the odd feeling of walking through the front door after spending a few days away and seeing what are normally familiar surroundings in a new and not altogether uncritical light. In that brief window of opportunity, which may last only minutes, the defects that time has taught us to overlook are often suddenly glaringly obvious. But some shortfalls and deficiencies take a while to reveal themselves. You may have to live in a house for a considerable period of time to realize how best to improve it or undergo several changes of lifestyle before reorganization becomes a pressing concern.

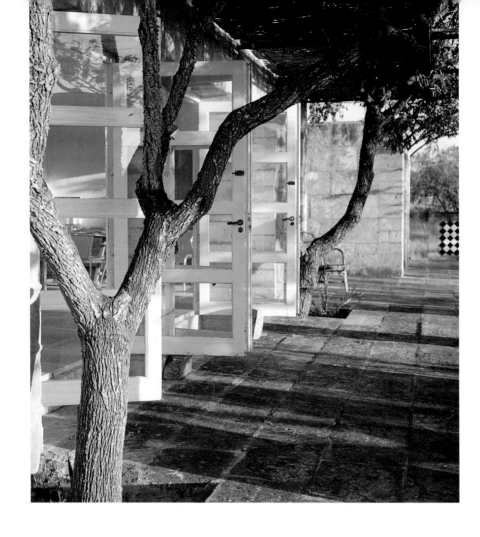

Thinking about basic elements represents a kind of mental paring down. But it does not necessarily entail the rarefied contemplation of minimalism. For dedicated minimalists, space, light, colour and texture are not merely basic elements, they are the only elements. In buildings designed to provide such purity and perfection, the focus is entirely abstract. Things, however ordinary, are banished or hidden. And paradoxically, whenever objects are brought out to be used, no matter how unprepossessing they are, they can assume an almost distracting significance in the absence of anything else to look at. The result may indeed induce a Zen-like sense of peace and calm, as enthusiasts maintain, but at the considerable price of living in surroundings that constantly tell you what to do. I cannot help but feel that minimalism offers the enforced calm of the straitjacket, not the sense of ease I would naturally associate with being 'at home'.

In the public imagination, the term 'minimal' has become somewhat interchangeable with 'modern'. This is not altogether surprising, since there are clearly certain common denominators. While minimalism may be an uncomfortably extreme position for most people, it does reveal, like the best of modern architecture, the often unsung beauty of the

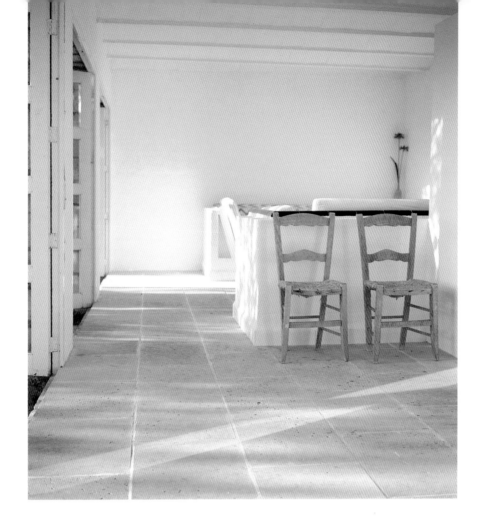

everyday – the play of natural light, the sheer dynamic of space and the subtleties of form and texture. Concentrating on these fundamentals is important, not least because they are so often overlooked. In the context of home design, many people tend to get obsessed by what is in the foreground, when the background may actually have a greater part to play. Realization often comes after the fact, when you can't think why you waited so long to make some simple alteration.

Minimalism offers another valuable insight, too, which is recognizing the irrelevance of a good deal of what fills our homes. Almost everyone could do with a little less in their lives. Here, a critical attitude is important to edit out what is surplus to requirements. This is not a case of making do with the bare minimum – unless you are that way inclined – but of weeding out what is redundant, ineffective or simply past the point where it is useful or meaningful.

There is a fine line that can be drawn between the clarity that modernism offers and the rather uptight nature of most minimal interiors. I've noticed that people who live in such formal surroundings have a tendency to rush off on holiday at the drop of a hat, searching, no doubt, for somewhere they can live a bit more easily. There's no denying that modern can be easy, but not if it results in the kind of visual tenseness where furniture, fittings and interior space all share the same tight and angular aesthetic. If minimalism looks like it's hard work, that's because it often is. The best modern interiors, on the other hand, are liberating rather than constraining, freeing time and the imagination and putting the individual back firmly in the centre of the picture.

Most people, perhaps, can more readily imagine easy living taking place in an older house. It seems to go naturally with well-worn floors, generously proportioned rooms, sunlight flooding through sash windows and robust finishes that display the gentle mellowing of age. Older houses offer the comfort of familiarity and a sense of connection with both nature and history, a sense that is increasingly threatened in other areas of life.

The spatial issues that arise from living in a home with a past are of a different nature to those presented by the modern interior. In this situation, the question is frequently how to reconcile architectural character with the demands of contemporary living. Period houses can arouse extreme emotions in people – either the desire to rip out all historical features and start anew, or the desire (much more common nowadays) to conserve or reproduce every minute detail down to the last fingerplate. Neither approach is particularly satisfactory. The former can be tantamount to vandalism; the latter forces you to live in an anachronism. Here, concentrating on the basic elements can help achieve a balance between an old framework and a modern lifestyle.

Buildings live longer than people and often outlast their original function, which makes an excessively preservationist attitude something of a nonsense. Subservience to the past can all too easily shade into pastiche and in the process what is truly timeless and appealing is lost. Loft living provides a good example of the benefits of creative transformation, bringing new life to perfectly serviceable structures – factories, schools, warehouses and so on – which would otherwise be redundant, and regenerating run-down areas of the inner city. In such cases, the answer is having the courage to combine old with new, marrying the depth of character that comes with the accretions of time with the sense of vitality that places you firmly in the here and now.

space

Without necessarily realizing it, we have an instinctive sense of proportion, derived from the natural world. In the 'Modulor' (above), a system of scale based on the dimensions of the human form, Le Corbusier attempted to provide a harmonious blueprint for design. The sweep of a stair and the vertical element of the column (left) have a natural echo in the towering uprights of the forest glade (right).

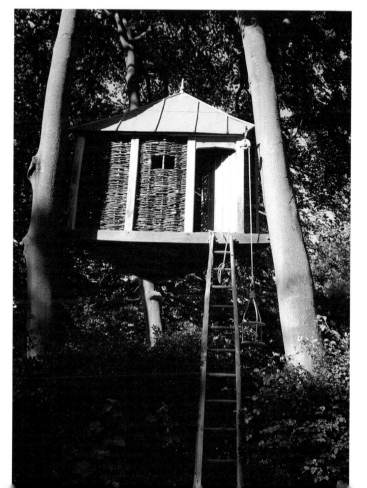

For most people, space means 'having enough room', as in space to put things or do things, or simply breathing space. The value of this increasingly precious commodity, however, cannot be measured merely in terms of quantity. What attracts us to certain spaces and not to others has more to do with abstract notions of proportion, balance and individual character than with the sheer elbow room of square feet and inches. The quality of space may be a concept that is difficult to articulate, but it plays a key role in our enjoyment of life.

Our attitudes to interior space are rooted in the natural world. It is not difficult to relate primitive shelters – tents, huts, tepees and igloos – to caves, groves of trees, caverns and other natural places of refuge. Not only are such vernacular structures typically built out of whatever materials are at hand; their scale and proportion often echo, whether consciously or not, natural harmonies.

The references to nature may be both literal and theoretical. The Greek temple, for example, has marble columns and lintels that have been carved to suggest earlier basic wooden forms of construction, while the orders of classical architecture are based on the 'golden section', where mathematical relationships can be found in the spiral form of galaxies, seashells, flowerheads and fir cones. The intuitive 'rightness' of such blueprints of design can be appreciated whether or not we have an understanding or even an awareness of the calculations. In the same way, the enduring appeal of symmetry can be traced to its familiarity as a pattern featuring prominently in nature.

It may seem an enormous leap from the hut to the high-rise apartment, but even modern architects, such as Le Corbusier, have attempted to base their designs on a natural system of scale. Le Corbusier's 'Modulor' took the human form as the basic index of dimension with the intention of bringing a universal harmony to design: 'proportion is the means to architectural lyricism' is how he termed it. We may not enter a room and subject it to that same intense level of analysis, but we know it when we feel it – when the basic proportion and disposition of space put us at our ease.

If spatial quality has much to do with a natural sense of proportion, it also provides a balance of emotional experience. Openness and enclosure, security and exhilaration, privacy and togetherness are all equally desirable and necessary.

At least part of the popularity of lofts and converted warehouses must be the fact that they offer the relatively rare opportunity to enjoy the almost giddy pleasure of life on a grand scale. When so much housing, old or new, has been designed to meagre spatial standards, finding yourself in a huge open expanse seems to promise infinite possibilities. Where such spaces are double-height, there is the added bonus of sweeping upward views, providing an uplifting sensation that normally one expects to experience only in public buildings and churches. It is this volume of space that generates the feeling of freedom, as much as the floor area.

Open space inspires a generous, inclusive approach to living. When barriers are down, activities can flow from one into another – from cooking to eating, from eating to relaxing – without the formal segregation implied by separate rooms. The planning of many of the houses we have inherited from the nineteenth century enshrine Victorian social distinctions between old and young, servants and masters, men and women, divisions that are no longer relevant or welcome. This strict spatial segregation also implies a hierarchy of activity, ranging from areas devoted to chores to areas set aside for near-indolence. Today, cooking may be work, but we expect it to be pleasurable work, part of the daily life of the whole household. Open space, whether it is achieved by converting an industrial building or knocking down walls in a Victorian terrace, allows everyone access to easy living.

Outdoor living areas restore a sense of connection with nature. With their elemental simplicity, the concrete table and benches sit easily in this garden (above).

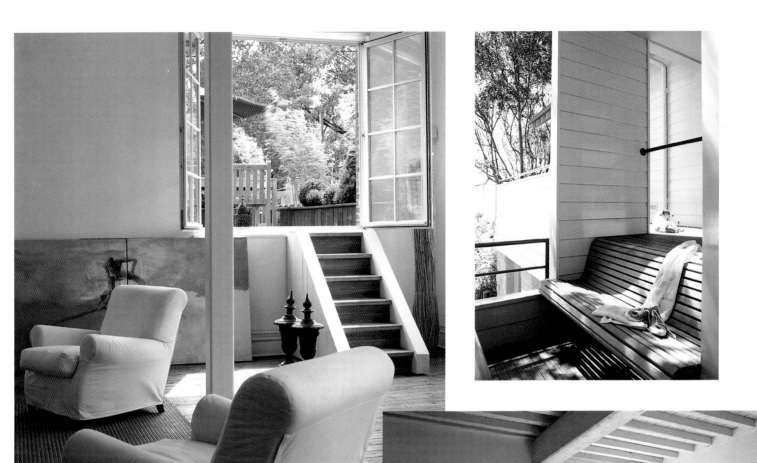

Yet, as anyone who has tried to live in a single vast space will tell you, people also need places that are small and enclosed. In a warehouse conversion, this might simply be a partitioned area where you can shut the door and be by yourself. In other contexts, the enclosures may be smaller still: the alcove, box bed, window seat or chimney corner are traditional spatial patterns with an irresistible appeal. Self-contained, compact, secure and private, such features may not be practically necessary in the strictest sense, but they are hugely enjoyable.

For spaces to come alive, there must also be a sense of progression. This depends to a large extent on views and vistas that change as one moves from area to area or level to level. The staircase is potentially one of the most dynamic architectural features in this respect, but there are other means to the same end.

Balconies and generous openings such as French windows dissolve the boundary between indoors and out, half enclosed but open to light and air.

Designed by Andrew Patterson, this house (below), **on a hill west of Auckland, New Zealand, has louvred panels that open fully to reveal the dramatic backdrop of a rugged landscape.**

Courtyards, mezzanine levels, skylights, glazed internal doors or windows that allow glimpses from room to room, and other visual links between one part of a space and another or between indoors and out all generate an immense sense of vitality.

Assessing spatial quality can be difficult, particularly when one is so accustomed to the sort of standardized domestic planning common to most Western housing. This difficulty may account, in part, for the current fascination with feng shui, the ancient Chinese discipline that prescribes all manner of correct spatial alignments and placings to ensure good health, happiness and fortune. At present, feng shui is enjoying the full panoply of cult status and is the subject matter of countless books, magazines, newspaper articles and television programmes, and providing work for any number of consultants; nevertheless, that should not detract from the basic insights it has to offer.

While I am not temperamentally inclined to subscribe to the mystic rationale behind the practice of feng shui – the appeasement of good spirits or energies, the warding off of evil eyes – I can still appreciate the way in which these rules encapsulate many centuries' worth of observations on the sensitivity of human beings to their surroundings. I am not certain, for example, that I would be prepared to live with the constant tinkling of a wind chime, but I can recognize the fact that

for a wind chime to tinkle, there must be airflow, and the flow of air through a room, as opposed to the static, sealed atmosphere of a double-glazed office, is entirely beneficial and pleasurable. In feng shui, orientation is very important, with the Chinese preferring a north–south site, which, of course, is the best position for benefiting from solar power. In the same way, feng shui practitioners place great stress on furniture arrangement, recommending that desks be placed so they face an open door – which, as anyone can sense, is psychologically the most comfortable spot. A strategically positioned mirror (what one writer has called the 'aspirin of feng shui') may perhaps redirect the flow of ch'i, but it undoubtedly multiplies views and light. Flowers and other living plants may be remedies for every type of conceivable misfortune, from sharp protruding corners to over-scaled windows, but they also soften an interior by acting as living reminders of the natural world.

What constitutes bad feng shui is no less commonsensical. Homes that are poorly serviced, in need of repair or badly maintained have bad feng shui; clutter clogging up cupboards, attics and lurking under the stairs is also unpropitious. Feng shui encompasses many rules, from broad principles down to fine-tuning, but perhaps its most valuable contribution is the holism of the basic premise: that the quality of space and how we arrange it has a fundamental impact on our well-being.

The free flow of space in this house in Ahmadabad, India (above and right), **designed by Le Corbusier, expresses perfectly his belief in the plan as the driving force in architectural design.**

The 'enfilade' or symmetrical sequence through a suite of rooms is a classic spatial arrangement, dramatically enhanced in Trivancore Palace, India by a glossy black floor – a finish achieved, apparently, with egg white (above, far left).

Older houses were generally planned to segregate activities, with rooms assigned specific functions. Removing dividing walls allows living areas to flow more informally (above left).

Volume – as much as floor space – creates a thrilling feeling of expansiveness. In this loft-like conversion (left), internal windows provide commanding views across the living area.

A mezzanine level inserted within a large converted space maintains a sense of openness while offering a degree of privacy for sleeping (above).

In open-plan spaces, the positioning of furniture is of critical importance, setting up focal points of activity and creating circulation routes from one area to the next. This dining 'room' (above right) is defined solely by the placement of the table, chairs and fixed lighting.

Relaxed and informal, this sympathetic updating of an older house manages to retain an appealing architectural quality while making the most of views and natural light (right).

light

Light, more than any other element of the interior, generates mood and atmosphere: it has a direct line to the emotions. Sight is our most highly developed sense, and it is not surprising that light, which renders the world visible, should have such a profound effect on the way we feel. Given its central importance, however, it is curious that only a fraction of the effort and expense devoted to other aspects of decoration and furnishing is spent on lighting the home. One reason may be the fact that lighting is commonly perceived to be a difficult and technical subject that few of us could even attempt to understand; another may be that people have a tendency to get distracted by the various styles of light fittings available rather than consider the quality of light itself. Many homes are still both badly lit and overlit, which very often amounts to the same thing.

As is the case with space, thinking about light directs our attention back to the natural world. Human beings are instinctively drawn to the light, instantly revitalized by sunny days and oppressed by overcast skies. The annual summer migration of northerners to the warmer climates of the south can be seen as a quest for light; the popularity of package

holidays reveals this to be a very powerful craving. The identification of SAD (seasonal affective disorder) shows how serious the effects of light deprivation can be.

Bright sunshine is not the only enjoyable form of natural light, though. If you sit out of doors in the garden for any length of time, particularly in a sheltered spot, you will experience a series of minute variations of light levels and intensity. There may be crisply defined shadows when the sun is overhead, soft lengthening shadows towards the end of the day, patterns of dappled light and shade where the sun shines through the leaves of a tree, golden subfusc light as the setting sun catches on tiny dust particles in the air. It is these variations, as much as the mere fact that the sun is shining at all, that give pleasure.

More dramatic changes in the weather can also make you 'see things in a different light' – such as the sudden and ominous darkening that precedes a thunderstorm. In the same way, you can often sense that it has snowed overnight without getting up to look out of the window – the bright glare reflected up from the snowy ground generates a completely different quality of light. In southern California, the atmospheric

The simplicity of the paper lantern belies its effectiveness as one of the most evocative diffusers of light (above, far left).

Light becomes 'bluer' at twilight (above centre). **Artificial lighting should complement natural light levels, not act as a substitute.**

Dappled light, with its constantly moving patterns of light and shadow, generates a mood of immense well-being (above).

Natural light is always changing in colour, level, direction and intensity, from a dramatic stormy sky (right) **to the soft, rosy light of dawn. Artificial lighting should also achieve such variety.**

changes associated with smoggy conditions have given rise to the term 'airlight' to describe a diffused, generalized brightness. *L'heure bleue*, the French term for twilight, encapsulates perfectly that transitory time when the colour of light shifts towards the cool end of the spectrum. Artists from Turner to Hockney, who have a heightened sensitivity to such things, have often been attracted to a particular area of the world for the sole reason that it offers a different quality of light and thus a different way of perceiving colour.

Yet, no matter how aware people are of these differences, from moment to moment or latitude to latitude, that variety of light is all too rarely duplicated indoors. In place of the mobility of natural light, there is often a fixed, static central focus; in place of diffusion and subtlety, there is glare, and instead of intriguing patches of light and shade, there is uniform brightness which cancels out all depth of character. It is as if artificial light is only seen as a practical tool, a second-rate substitute for sunshine, with no aesthetic impact at all. Much more useful and ultimately more rewarding is to consider the quality of light in the interior overall, with natural and artificial sources working in partnership, which they do for much of the day and into the evening.

Living in northern latitudes, it is easy to assume that the more natural light a room receives the better — months of low winter sun and rainy weather make one greedy for as much sunlight as possible. It is no accident, for example, that Scandinavian styles of decorating seem designed to maximize the light, with pale airy colours, uncluttered windows and plenty of clear floor space. On the other hand, in areas of the world with more reliable weather, strong daylight, which can heat up an interior to an uncomfortable degree, is not as welcome. In warmer southern countries, there are wide verandas or shaded terraces to create temperate zones between indoors and out, smaller windows with deep embrasures to cut down the sun's penetrating glare, and screens, lattices and awnings to filter the brightness.

But attitudes to light are not necessarily determined simply by location; taste also has a part to play. It is striking that in eighteenth-century Europe, when developments in

Light reveals texture and form. Strong directional light casts crisp, defining shadows; gentle diffused side-lighting emphasizes the material quality of different surfaces.

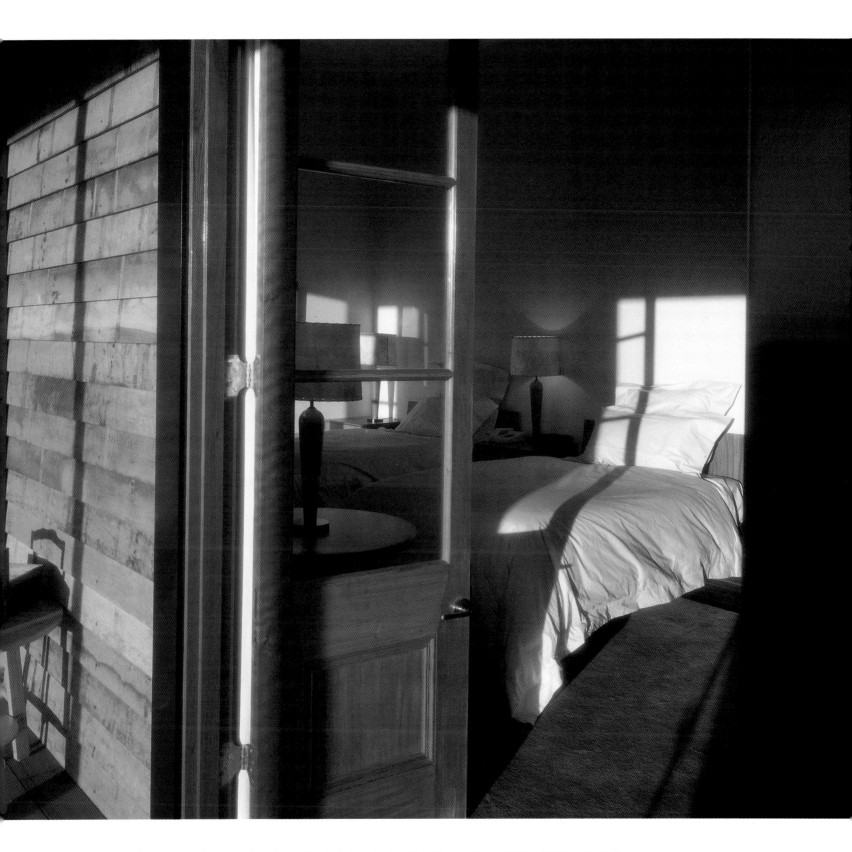

As devotees of feng shui advocate, orientation can have a profound effect on the way you feel. Being awakened by sunlight is a gentler and more natural way of starting the day than by the shrill summons of an alarm clock.

technology and construction introduced the means to create large window openings fitted with relatively clear glass, houses were flooded with light and decorated in sympathy, while a mere century later, Victorian homes were characterized by a heavy gloom, with sombre colour schemes, heavy furnishings, windows shrouded in layers of fusty drapery and natural light treated almost as an intruder. Of course, gaslight, candles and oil lamps did dirty and darken rooms very quickly, and it was not until the advent of electricity that houses began to lighten up again; this clean source of power meant that for the first time paler decorating schemes could stay pristine for far longer periods of time.

For most of us today, light is the flip side of the spatial coin. We need space around us to appreciate the effects of light and we need light to reveal space. Travel to very different climates has also given us a taste for what bright light can do, and the result is a desire to make the most of whatever light is available at home. This can be achieved very simply by paying attention to orientation, so that activities benefiting from daylight take place in those areas of the home more likely to receive it. Enlarging or creating new windows and keeping window treatments unfussy will allow as much light as possible to be admitted; choosing the right colours and finishes will spread the light around and reflect it.

Such strategies for maximizing the effects of natural light are more or less obvious. It is natural light's partner – artificial lighting – that has a tendency to create more difficulties. When it was first made available to homes in the late nineteenth century, electrical lighting was perceived as extremely bright, although wattages were a fraction of what they are today. Since then, homes have been getting brighter and brighter, while at the same time, the number of light sources has decreased.

The end result is often an uncomfortable glare and a uniformity of effect that can be extremely oppressive. Glare is the antithesis of easy living, and for very good physical reasons. It occurs when there is too great a contrast between a source of light and its surroundings, meaning that the eye has to make continual and unpleasant adjustments between the two. Uniformity – where all distinctions are flattened – is merely depressing.

Artificial lighting does not have the same in-built variations that natural light has and which makes it so appealing. No matter how much natural light a room receives, the effect will never be static, simply because the colour, direction and intensity of light are changing constantly as the sun makes it way across the sky. When you are creating an artificial lighting scheme, you have to work that much harder to provide an equivalent richness of experience.

In northern latitudes, where there can be many months of grey skies, we need as much natural light in the interior as possible. High-level arched windows flood the space with pure light in this house designed by the minimalist architect Claudio Silvestrin (above).

Much can be done simply by increasing the number of light sources in a room, at the same time decreasing the intensity of each light. One bright ceiling light may well supply all the light you need to see by, but it will not provide the right quality of light to live by. A variety of dimmer light sources at different heights and angled in different directions, on the other hand, is immediately comfortable and atmospheric. Each light on its own is not bright enough to hurt the eyes, but the sum total of illumination is still the same. And in place of a flat, even level of light, there are overlapping pools of brightness and shade that enhance form and texture. It may be light that we are drawn to, but it is shadow that makes things interesting.

Direction of light is another key factor. Light upwards – so that light bounces off the ceiling – and you create a sense of expansion. Light sideways, and you graze surfaces, revealing contour and texture. Light downwards

and you pick out a page, a keyboard, a worktop or an object in a tight focus of attention. Combine some or all of these in one particular area and you begin to create a sense of vitality.

The enormous range of light sources that are now on the market also enables you to experiment with colour. Tungsten, which is certainly still the most common of all domestic light sources, gives off a warm, golden cast that is inherently domestic. It is also more than a little familiar, as it comes most closely to matching the colour of candlelight.

In recent years, halogen lighting has become far more widely available for use in the home. Crisp and white

and with the ability to render colours nearly as faithfully as daylight, halogen introduces yet another dimension to the lighting repertoire. Adding a dimmer system to such lights also gives you the option of changing the mood and quality of light still further as early evening shades into dark night.

In the context of lighting, what works aesthetically is not far removed from what works on a practical basis. Good functional light is glare-free and often directional. It illuminates the task at hand without shining in your eyes or causing distracting reflections on the periphery. It is bright enough, but not over-bright. And like all forms of servicing, it is only as good as its infrastructure. Flexibility is that much easier to achieve when there are enough power points and well-positioned controls.

Quality of light is critical for easy living. Whether it is the midday sun slanting through half-closed venetian blinds, the warm, intimate circle of light spilling from a shaded table lamp, the boost to concentration from an angled work lamp, the hospitality of dancing firelight and flickering candlelight, or the dappled light of a shaded veranda or terrace, light is one of the most engaging of basic elements.

Warm light is reassuring, intimate and hospitable. Firelight is as warm psychologically as it is physically, while the golden light of dusk completely saturates colours. Tungsten light, which has a rich golden cast similar to candlelight, is both welcoming and flattering.

Rooms with more than one aspect, where natural light comes from different directions, have an innate sense of vitality (below). The effect is especially pronounced if windows are on adjacent, rather than opposite, walls. As the sun changes position in the sky, the level and direction of light shift accordingly.

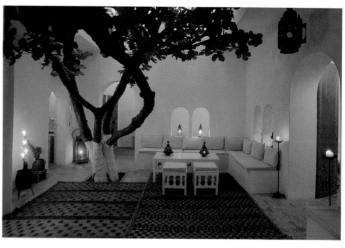

Colour is a key consideration when planning a lighting scheme. Halogen light sources have a cool, white tone, similar to daylight, while tungsten, the standard domestic light source, and candlelight are much warmer and more intimate.

The success of a lighting scheme depends on having a number of different light sources, setting up contrasting pools of light and shadow to lead the eye from point to point. Each source need not be very bright, but the final effect will be efficient and atmospheric. In this home (left), bright, focused lighting is aimed at the kitchen worktop, with more intimate, shaded lamps positioned alongside the sofas. Concealed lighting – essential for avoiding glare – picks out the staircase and bookshelves.

It can be a challenge in an open-plan space to reconcile the different levels of light needed for various moods and activities. Here, a Perspex panel makes a diffusing screen that softens the brighter light in the kitchen area and forms a gentle backdrop to the living space (right).

colour

On the face of it, colour seems to be far less complex an issue than either space or light. Colour, after all, is self-evident; it speaks for itself. Yet few decisions appear to cause more anxiety or inspire more soul-searching than choosing colours to live with. Those who are otherwise fairly confident in their selection of basic furnishings and products, able to weigh up the pros and cons of practicality, cost and style, often find that their minds go completely blank when confronted by a paint chart. It is at this point when retreat into neutrality seems the safest option.

Other cultures do not share our hesitancy. Wherever the light is strong, there are dazzling combinations of colour – from hundreds of Mediterranean variations on the theme of blue to the electric clashing colours of Africa, Asia and Latin America. Exposure to such palettes, through travel or colour photography, have at least shown us what we are missing. Purists might insist that bright colours do not travel well without the bright light that accompanies them; but such a stance seems to ignore the incredibly vibrant colours often found in northern vernacular buildings – the farmhouses of southwest Ireland, for example – while at the same time condemning us to living with appropriately tweedy shades. I do not see any reason why the colours you encounter on holiday should not inspire you at home, encapsulating a memory of a favourite place.

Colour, these days, is big business, more readily available, affordable and achievable than at any other time in history. In the past, certain bright colours – for example, a reliable bright yellow – were technically impossible to produce from the animal, vegetable and mineral sources that were the basis of most pigments. Others, notably the pure blue derived from lapis lazuli, were astronomically expensive. It is the rarity and exclusivity of this blue that accounts for its widespread appearance as the colour of the robes of the Virgin Mary in early paintings. Strong colour, of course, was not unknown in previous centuries and it is often surprising to discover

how bright many historical interiors actually were – many people nowadays would run shuddering from an original freshly painted Adam interior. But for ordinary households in the past, the everyday palette was far more muted, with interior colours, in particular, closely associated with commonly used building materials. There were woody shades used on woodwork and stony colours used on walls; service rooms and passageways were often painted all-purpose 'drab' – the pale greyish-brown achieved by mixing the dregs.

Today, compared to our ancestors, we are spoiled for choice. Yet when we can have all the bright yellow and pure blue we want, why does magnolia, the contemporary incarnation of drab, remain such a popular choice? Why do we find it so difficult to know what we really like?

I suspect that the breadth of choice available to us may be part of the problem. Another related aspect is that as the hectic cycles of fashion invade interior design and decoration – the 'brown is the new black' mentality – it seems both too bewildering and too exhausting to keep up. One minute lime-green saturates the style pages and the next minute it is orange or pale lavender. It does not take much to figure out that responding to colour trends in your home would mean you were rarely without a paintbrush in your hand.

I believe, however, that such inhibitions are worth overcoming. Even if it were possible to rule out colour completely (and some people have a good try), it would be profoundly depressing. Colour adds flavour to life. Using it positively and learning how to assess the way it makes you feel adds richness to the way you experience your surroundings and can become a major component of easy living.

Colour is visceral. But while you may love or hate a colour instantly, the reasons for such a response may be rather more complex than you think. Cultural associations can be powerful. Asians, for example, marry in red and mourn in white.

Green, which falls in the part of the spectrum that our eyes see most easily, is inherently restful and soothing.

Colour is detail in this minimalist interior. Incidental objects – such as flowers, paintings,
even people – can all provide vivid accents when the backgrounds are pure or neutral.

Vivid cushions provide a visual treat and a human touch in a restrained modern interior (right).

All dyes originally came from natural sources, whether animal, vegetable or mineral (above). Natural dyes can result in tones as soft as the earthy flecks of tweed or as searing as the vibrant hues of India. Textiles that have been dyed or coloured naturally fade gracefully with time and repeated washing.

The inspiration for colour is everywhere: the landscape, flowers and even food can all be the starting point when choosing colours to live with.

Colour depends on context, in particular the conditions of natural light. Coloured glass is particularly evocative as it dapples surfaces with intensely coloured shadows.

Nature provides many surprising colour
combinations; the patterns on the wings of
butterflies were my childhood passion.

Red is the luckiest colour for the Chinese, symbolizing happiness and strength, while yellow means long life. Feng shui practitioners regard all-white rooms as invitations to disaster; what we might find chic and sophisticated, they believe encourages serious illness. We ascribe our own positive and negative emotions to colours: red is for anger, debt and seduction; green for envy and 'go'; yellow for cowardice and constancy; blue for purity, freshness and depression. Designers of packaging and logos pay extremely close attention to such meanings, and manufacturers and retailers profit by them.

On the purely physical side, we have in-built sensitivities to certain colours which derive from wavelength patterns. In daylight conditions, our eyes naturally find colours in the middle of the spectrum – from yellow to green – easiest to see. Green, therefore, is literally relaxing and restful, whether it is the green of a garden or landscape or the pale green on the walls of an operating theatre where it provides the least distracting environment for life-or-death surgery. As daylight begins to fade, the range in which we see most easily shifts slightly to blue. Red, on the other hand, is anything but restful. While blue is the colour of coolness and distance, red is warm and advancing. It is both nature's alarm bell and lure, signalling the poisonous berry and the ripe apple; it stimulates action. It will grab a baby's attention as quickly as a shopper's.

How the perception of colour is affected by light and, in turn, how colour affects our perception of space, is critical when it comes to decorating and furnishing the home. Pale colours, which have a lot of white in them, reflect light and spread it around; dark colours, on the other hand, are more enclosing and light-absorbent. But a great deal depends on context. Blue, for example, can be airy and inspirational, its distancing effect increasing the sense of spaciousness. However, in a room that receives little direct sunlight, the same shade can appear cold, clinical and downright depressing. Red can be warm, welcoming and cheerful, but in large doses it is simply exhausting, too much of a good thing.

Certain shades that hover on the brink between one colour and the next, such as blue-green, grey-blue, orangey-red and reddish-blue, change dramatically at different times of the day – luminous variations that can be a useful way of

**Blue is the colour of distance and expansion –
think of the sea and the sky. In the interior, it has
the effect of increasing the sense of spaciousness,
but it needs to be used in areas where the quality of
natural light is good, otherwise the effect can be
clinical and enervating. Here, blue defines a kitchen
wall in a space well lit by a glazed roof** (centre).
**By contrast, red is an advancing colour that attracts
the attention and adds vitality. What might be tiring
on a grand scale makes an unbeatable accent.**

introducing a sense of vitality to your surroundings. Picking
out a component of one of these hybrid shades to use as
an accent, for example setting blue against reddish-blue,
often has an invigorating edginess, while pale grey-blue
backgrounds seem to make other colours sing out. What are
properly termed complementary colours, that is those that sit
opposite each other on the colour wheel, such as red and
green or blue and orange, tend to make stimulating
partnerships. Studying colour theory is one route to such
discoveries; even better is taking the trouble to look – at
nature, in particular. My boyhood passion for moths and
butterflies introduced me to unimaginable combinations of
colour and pattern as did my ambition to collect and press
every wild flower in the land. I couldn't have had a better
introduction to the impact of colour contrast than that offered
by one of my earliest colour memories – seeing bright green
paint spilled on a terracotta-tiled floor.

It is important to remember that rooms can be colourful even when the walls are painted white – perhaps the commitment implied by painting all four walls the same shade is part of what scares people off in the first place. Joseph, the fashion entrepreneur, loves colour, but believes that mixing different colours successfully is actually a very difficult skill to master. Rather than make a mistake, he keeps the backgrounds in his home soft and muted, neutral tones against which the vibrant shades of flowers, fruit and clothing can stand out. The spines of books, a painted door, plastic beakers, intriguing packaging, coloured glass vases, cushions and throws, flowers, paintings, even people in the room can contribute substantial jolts of colour, visual treats that the eye returns to again and again – and that's my philosophy on colour, too. Colour, in this sense, can just happen, and the result is often far more refreshing and joyous than the most carefully planned and coordinated scheme.

Texture alters our perception of colour. Rugged, matt or grainy surfaces tone down the intensity of different shades, while glossy, polished or reflective surfaces add definition and vibrancy. Natural materials, such as wood, terracotta and rough plaster, come in an inherently gentle palette of earthy, companionable tones, all of which work well together.

texture

Texture connects us with the physical world where materials have weight and resistance, surface and finish. In the pattern of grain or drape of a cloth, texture acts as a reminder of how things are made, by man and by nature.

In the context of interior design, the visual importance of texture is widely stressed. Texture, as a variable of colour, can soften or sharpen a tone – you only have to consider the contrasting impact of matt, satin and gloss paint finishes.

As an intrinsic element of pattern, texture emphasizes movement and rhythm, evident in the direction of a weave or the twist of a pile. In fact, it is arguable that patterns that have some foundation in texture, such as damask and brocade, have more inherent vitality than those that are simply surface-printed. Variations between smooth and rough and ridged and plain introduce a sense of definition and character, revealed as light is reflected off the surface of the fabric, or shadows fall into hollows and indentations. The simpler the surroundings, and the more subdued the colours, the greater the role that texture has to play.

But what texture can do for the appearance of a room is only a part of the story. Seeing is not always believing, which explains why we like to squeeze fruit on a market stall, finger the nap of a suit hanging on a shop-rail or stroke the surface of a sofa. Texture always implies and invites touch, from the tips of the fingers to the soles of the feet; the tactility of the materials we live with contributes profoundly to the pleasure we derive from using them. A polished wooden banister, an earthenware pot, painted brickwork, a nubbly rug, a scrubbed oak table and a porcelain cup may all share the same neutral tones, but they offer widely different experiences the minute they are encountered directly.

Variations of texture add character and tactility to this interior (right). **The smooth spindles of the chair backs invite touch, as do the terracotta urn and woven objects, placed where the light reveals the quality of their surfaces.**

Wood grain, evident in unfinished beams and columns or in smooth veneer, has a direction and pattern that serve as a reminder of the living origin of the material.

Hard, reflective metal panels, appliances and door fronts sharpen the look of working areas like kitchens. Metal brings a chic contemporary edge to the home, borrowed from industrial contexts such as factories and laboratories – though nature, too, offers a similar palette of colours.

Natural materials age well, acquiring a pleasing

character over years of handling and use.

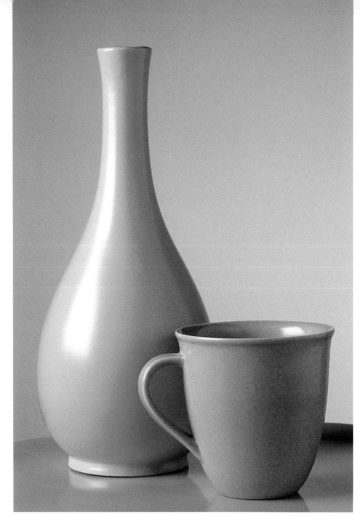

Texture draws in other senses, too. The hollow echo of floorboards when you walk on them, the chink of glass, the rustle of silk are the aural evidence of material quality. Here, as in other areas, sensations overlap: the clubby smell of leather is indivisible from the warm grainy feel of hide; the sharp tang of new wood is as instantly identifiable as whorls and knotholes.

On this sensual, emotional level, contrast is also critical. An environment that was seamless and smooth would be curiously dislocating and other-worldly, while one that was entirely rough and unyielding we would naturally read as a fairly hostile place – you only have to compare the experience of walking in a natural landscape with walking in a shopping mall or along an asphalted road. Real terrain offers a rich variety of experience underfoot, from dry, shifting leaves to bouncy turf, from the slow drag of sand to the tense grip of rock. Uniform urban environments, such as relentlessly smooth terrazzo or concrete, tire the mind as much as the feet.

Of equal importance is that textural variety can satisfy our innate desire for change and stimulation without setting thoughts flying in every direction. An excess of visual distraction, where everything is clamouring for attention – too many colours, too much clutter, too much decorative detail – can all too quickly send you into overload. Variety of surface and finish, however, is far more insinuating and subtle; it registers on a less conscious plane.

If texture is a way of grounding everyday experience, it also provides a way of authenticating materials. I am not a huge fan of synthetic products, even though I can appreciate the vibrant, luminous colours and organic forms that can be achieved in plastics, and relish their use for their own sake. In general, however, mass market synthetics always seem to be a bit of a cheat, promising a look-alike quality without the more tangible dimensions of the real thing. The deception is for your eyes only. You only have to walk on a vinyl floor or touch marbleized tiles or sleep in polyester sheets or eat off a laminate table to notice the difference. The floor will sound tinny, the tiles will be warm to the touch, the sheets will not breathe and the tabletop will be scratchy.

What I dislike most about artificial materials is their inability to age in any agreeable way. Real, natural materials, derived from plants, animals or the earth, seem to retain the same ability to change that one associates with living things.

Textural quality contributes profoundly to the pleasure we derive from everyday activities. The smoothness of glass and porcelain makes tumblers and cups a delight to hold and sip from, just as a polished banister invites you to run your hand along it. The subtle textural contrasts of wood, stainless steel and stone flooring offer a variety of tactile, acoustic and visual experiences – differences that register on an almost subconscious level but which are no less important for being unemphatic.

The ageing process, provided there is a degree of care and maintenance, is always for the better. Connoisseurs of antique furniture wax lyrical about patina, the depth and character that comes of years of sympathetic handling, care and use; it is rather difficult to imagine synthetic products, which either stubbornly refuse to grow old, or do so in the most unappealing way, attracting such a degree of affection in decades to come, although I have to admit that sixty-year-old Bakelite does appear to have achieved cult status.

Texture is the most obvious way such distinctions are conveyed. A flagged floor, worn by the relentless tread of feet, linen sheets repeatedly washed to a silky softness, solid tabletops scrubbed and polished, smooth beachstones battered by the tide – all enshrine the passage of time, a continuity that is deeply reassuring and comfortable. I would never decry the new, or surround myself, as some people do, only with objects that have a respectably long pedigree. But materials that have this in-built capacity to wear well and grow old gracefully seem to me to be the essence of easy living, simply because they are so inherently tolerant. Fading from the sun, and all the other gentle discolorations and marks of time tend to inspire

affection rather than revulsion. When the material has a natural source, it's easy to put up with such minor imperfections, even grow to like them, and where everything shares the same capacity to mellow, the overall effect is bound to be sympathetic. By contrast, materials that trick you at the essential point of contact and unnervingly shrug off all signs of use or require constant vigilance to maintain their pristine condition add work, stress and a sense of unreality to your life. Although they are often promoted as labour-saving, the very reverse is often the case. It is also important to consider that synthetic materials are at their best on day one and can go downhill fairly rapidly thereafter.

Textural quality, and indeed variety, require a certain investment of time and money. Natural materials are usually more expensive than their synthetic counterparts, whose economy is often their most persuasive selling point. Real, natural materials can also be demanding in terms of care and maintenance, although it must be said that the effort expended in this regard is always repaid by a pleasing renewal of character and finish. Such choices are to be made for the economic long run and for your long-term contentment.

This house in Ahmadabad, India (left), designed by Le Corbusier, reveals a masterful play of surface and finish, with exposed brick walls contrasting with the dramatic grid of local stone flooring. Textural quality is often associated with vernacular buildings, where materials are natural in origin and sourced locally, such as whitewashed stone and brickwork, timber panelling and cladding; these materials can also be used to add character to more contemporary settings.

comfort

Comfort is one of those concepts that comes more sharply into focus when looked at the other way round — we all know what discomfort is. A couple of stops down from the acute emergency of pain, discomfort is water seeping into your shoes, crumbs in the bed, a nagging ache somewhere unimportant, a nasty draught, a noxious smell, a filthy taste, a sticky social situation . . . . Rooted in the physical, but not exclusively of the body, discomfort signals any kind of imperfect fit between ourselves and our surroundings.

Absence of comfort is not life-threatening. Indeed, whole centuries have passed without people giving it much thought, being for the most part rather more preoccupied with the stark realities of getting enough to eat or, at the top of the social scale, with simply showing off. Comfort did not begin to be designed into our lives until there was enough leisure to enjoy it. The court of Louis XV saw the introduction of the first upholstered furniture, padded, curved and angled to accommodate the human frame in repose, while at a similar time in England the notion of comfort became identified with a whole culture of domestic contentment. Comfort has had these two sides, tangible and intangible, ever since.

Perhaps it is something to do with the Protestant work ethic, or simply the lingering traces of a puritanical sensibility, but many people still regard comfort as something of an indulgence, the soft option that tempts you from the straight and narrow. I would argue that truly comfortable surroundings, where the lighting is set at just the right level, possessions are within easy reach, furniture supports your body and everything functions as it should, provide the best environment for creativity. This is not a view, I know, that is shared by many artists and writers who firmly uphold the belief that the garret life is essential for inspiration.

Comfort is a notoriously elastic term and inherently subjective, which may be part of the problem. If you consider basic physical parameters, for example something as seemingly specific as a comfortable temperature, it's hard to get two people to agree, even when they live under the same roof. One will always be turning up the heating or pulling on a jumper, while the other is opening an window and complaining how hot it is. It is the same with broader notions of comfort. Everyday life is unquestionably more comfortable today than it was in the distant past; indeed, we now take quite a high degree of comfort for granted. Few people in the West expect to have to break the ice in a washbasin first thing on a winter's morning, for example, or to sleep on a lumpy straw mattress. Comfort in this sense is also comparative, a way stage on the route between necessity and luxury.

Can you have too much of a good thing? Where comfort is taken as read, discomfort can suddenly seem more meaningful, even worthier, a sort of grit in the oyster theory. Perhaps I just don't like to feel uncomfortable if I can avoid it, but it seems to me that there is only a short step from believing that comfort somehow gets in the way of thinking about higher things and putting on a hair-shirt. Certainly, the degree of indulgence that swaddles, cocoons or insulates the senses can so easily lull you into a near-vegetative state; pulling back from such overprotection may be the only way to remind yourself that you are still alive. But, again, it comes back to the way you define it. I see comfort less in terms of an extra cushion or slightly softer pillow and more as a state of equilibrium, a balance that is ultimately as liberating for work and self-expression as it is naturally pleasurable. For Joseph, too, comfort is a balance: 'Everything has got to be very relaxed but at the same time not so loose that one doesn't care.'

In the popular imagination, comfort is often confused with luxury. As architectural critic Jonathan Glancey pointed out in a recent article, 'luxury' is an appendage that is increasingly tagged on to a huge range of incredibly ordinary items in an attempt to persuade people to buy things they don't need or to persuade people that the things they do buy are exceptionally distinguished. I very much prefer his definition of luxury: '. . . a walk along a deserted beach . . . a house with stone floors in the heat of an Italian summer . . . having a day to yourself reading a book . . . lying in bed on a working day, rain beating against the window, a pot of tea and a pile of magazines and newspapers . . . .' And, of course, a cigar.

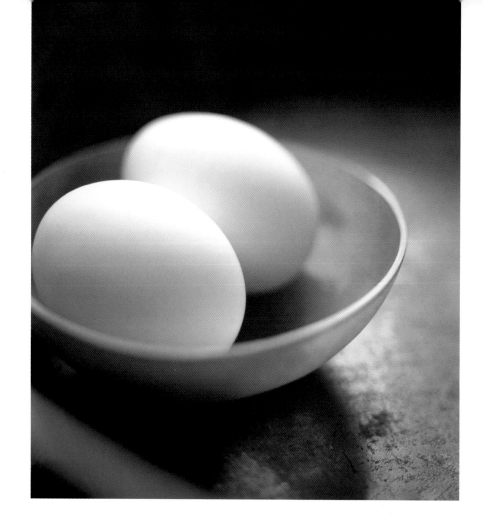

What makes the chef John Torode feel most comfortable is being able to sit down and read a book with his children, or working hard in the garden; it is definitely not the boring regimentation of the comfort zone 'where you are lounging in a chair reading the papers between the hours of nine and ten on a Sunday morning'. For Suzie Slesin, the design editor of the American magazine *House & Garden*, it is having 'no hands-off places' so that you don't have to worry constantly about something breaking or getting dirty.

Our daily lives are full of stress, much of which is unavoidable. I believe that if our homes cannot provide some kind of refuge or respite from that stress, both physically and emotionally, then they have failed in one of their most critical functions. From supporting the body at rest or during relaxation – physical comfort at its most basic – to elemental pleasures that put people at their ease, comfort provides a necessary sense of renewal. For me, comfort is neither mindless luxury nor suffocating indulgence: it is the essential breathing space in which we can simply be ourselves, surrounded by the things we really like rather than the things we think give us status.

relax

Providing a place to relax is one of the most important functions a home can fulfil today. The speed of communications, the frustrating slowness of traffic, the incessant intrusion of stimuli from television, phones, newspapers and computer networks mean that many people find themselves on constant alert. Days filled with appointments that shade into evenings answering phone messages and juggling commitments have little slack in them. But you cannot live in a state of battle-readiness for ever. When it all gets too much, and preferably well before breaking point, you need to recharge your batteries, take stock – or, in the French phrase, *reculer pour mieux sauter*: 'pull back to leap further'.

It takes time to unwind and when time is limited, you need all the help you can get to find the mental and physical room to let go. Spaces designed, arranged and furnished for easy living won't necessarily unclutter your diary, but they may keep you sane. The shift of gears into more comfortable surroundings acts as a kind of daily 'downshifting', a reminder that there are other ways of looking at things.

In theory, you should be able to relax almost anywhere in the home, but curiously the room that should provide the right environment for relaxation often conspicuously fails in this department. If you do most of your living away from the living room, something is going wrong somewhere.

Ghosts of former roles haunt many living rooms today. In the rigid hierarchy of Victorian society, the parlour was a public receiving room, decorated and furnished to impress. Well into this century, it was not uncommon for the sitting room or 'front room' to be kept more or less sealed until the next visitor arrived – in some households, it took a birth, wedding or funeral for the room to be opened to view. As a showcase, the sitting room was a place for prized possessions, wedding presents and the best furnishings a family could afford, but the trouble was that hardly anyone ever got to see them, much less use them. They were there primarily as a marker of status.

Living rooms are rarely kept under wraps these days – who could afford to lose so much space? – but something of this formal, hands-off status-seeking quality often lingers.

Comfort implies mental and physical breathing space – and that means surroundings where you can unwind, be yourself and spend at least some time doing very little of consequence. In a café near the Champs-Elysées, I once watched an elderly lady order a pear for dessert and then proceed to pare it slowly and expertly with a knife until the skin uncurled in a single spiral – a delicate performance of dexterity and concentration that must have been as relaxing to execute as it was to observe.

It is impossible to relax in rooms where furnishings require constant vigilance to remain in pristine condition or where everything says 'don't touch'. In this simple Australian house (left), **once the home of my daughter Sophie and her husband Alex Willcock, flagstone flooring, rammed earth walls and a raftered ceiling make a basic background, domesticated by a vivid chequered quilt hanging on the wall, natural fibre matting and white loose covers. My own home in the south of France** (right) **is also a converted farmhouse, where the simplicity of the stone flooring and plain whitewashed walls has been tempered by a layer of comfort in the form of cushions, throws and a rug.**

Although we may live in a much looser and more democratic culture today, it seems we haven't quite tamed our desire to show off. I think that rooms furnished with an eye to what the neighbours will think often end up being places no one enjoys very much. Keeping up appearances generates a kind of starchy atmosphere, which is far from comfortable; yet, ironically, the very last thing most people want, either for themselves or their guests, is to feel uneasy.

Rooms that are sending out all the wrong messages are one thing, but in many living areas the messages are far from clear. We know what kitchens and bathrooms are used for and the bedroom's role is self-evident. But, in many homes, living rooms simply accommodate what is left over, mopping up a series of activities and objects that may be entirely unrelated and fundamentally incompatible. Far from being

a place to relax, the living room turns into a zone that requires constant mediation. Here, there are two approaches you can take. You can be ruthless, decide what you really want the space to provide and replan your home so that all those objects that don't fit into the scheme of things go elsewhere or are disposed of. Alternatively, you can open the space up further, so that a natural flow of activity can take place. After all, it can be just as relaxing to cook a meal as to listen to music, and in an open-plan area there is no reason why you can't do both. Such spaces are inherently welcoming, because they offer the hospitable sense of being drawn into the life of the household.

How then do you set about creating relaxing and welcoming surroundings? The first step is being able to recognize exactly what it is that makes you feel at ease.

If I were to imagine the type of room that would make me feel comfortable and completely relaxed, it would contain a big, squashy sofa upholstered in creamy white, roomy wicker chairs with large, crumpled cushions and a well-worn stone floor covered with a beautiful rug. White linen curtains would flutter gently at open windows, admitting shafts of sunlight and wonderful views – the sea or a river in one direction and a lush green landscape in the other. There would be a fire in the fireplace, logs barely alight, so that the smell of woodsmoke drifted through the room. A carafe of wine, generous tumblers and a big bowl of French breakfast radishes would be set out on a scrubbed wooden table, and a large Morris Louis would be hung on the wall. I would be dressed in faded worn clothes (no tie) and a pair of my favourite leather slippers (no socks).

Those are the sort of surroundings that would please me. It stands to reason that if you please yourself, you are far more likely to make others feel welcome and comfortable, too, and the result will be the opposite of a room that puts everyone on their best behaviour. Comfortable seating, the right level of lighting and enough space to move around freely are obviously parts of the equation. And, since informality goes hand in hand with outdoor living, some connection with garden areas will bring in a spirit of freshness and vitality. On warm days, you want to be able to open windows and doors and venture out as the mood strikes. Furnishings that are equally at home indoors or out are not only inherently simple, they underscore this sense of connection.

In the city, we spend much of the time in a state of defensiveness, closing our ears to the blare of traffic, trying not to breathe in polluting fumes and turning our eyes away from the harsher sights of the urban environment. Relaxing means learning to let the barriers come down. Outdoor living provides the surest shortcut to re-engaging with the physical world and finding pleasure in it again; nature is unsurpassed in its ability to calm us down. A hammock slung between the branches of a tree, a simple table set up under vine-covered trellis, a garden seat surrounded by scented planting, a few fat cushions and a blanket thrown down in a grassy spot offer a directness of experience that is a real clue to easy living and well worth emulating inside the home.

The sounds, smells and sights we enjoy in nature provide valuable clues for creating the relaxing and comfortable spaces in which to live. One of the most soothing sounds that I know is the trickle of water in a garden pool.

Creative daydreaming can help
identify the situations and places
that make you feel the most
relaxed. The sound of running
water or waves breaking on the
shore is incredibly relaxing,
which may help to explain why
fishing is such a popular sport.
Although it would be impossible,
not to mention undesirable, to
divert a trout stream through
your living room, it is important
to pay attention to the quality
of sound and to make the most
of opportunities to connect
indoors with out.

Relaxing outdoors can be as basic as lying on a blanket under a shady tree or rocking gently in a hammock, while some of the most pleasant places of all are those indoor/outdoor areas, such as verandas and terraces, that are half-sheltered and half-exposed. Inside, there is no reason why rooms for relaxing should not display the same spontaneity and informality.

While few of us would want to install a fountain in the living room, it is important to pay attention to the quality of sound. Uniformly hard surfaces will result in a clattering environment full of grating noise, where the smallest movement is amplified to an uncomfortable degree, while heavily carpeted spaces, layered in fabric, have the muffled, deadened feel of a padded cell – the absence of sound can be strangely unnerving. A balance between resonant surfaces and finishes and sound-insulating ones, plus plenty of airflow to stir and rustle create an aural environment that is stimulating without being overwhelming.

Smell, our most evocative sense, is no less influential in shaping our mood. A scent is fleeting; it is estimated that we specifically notice all but the most pungent and noxious odours for mere seconds following our first exposure to them, after which time, we simply get used to them. This accounts for the critical importance of the threshold as a zone for enticing consumers into a shop, restaurant or supermarket; in some enterprises, appetizing smells of freshly baked bread and roast coffee are now synthesized and piped to strategic points to encourage spending – even new luxury cars are now sprayed with the smell of leather. At a time when fresh food is commonly sold sealed in layers of plastic, grown for appearance not flavour or aroma, and baking takes place in a distant factory, this seems exceptionally depressing and cynical to me. A good smell should be evidence of authenticity and quality; when we set out to analyse the particular smell of The Conran Shop, we found it to come from products, such as coffee, soap and wooden tables rubbed with linseed oil, that we were actually selling. In the home, too, the smells that greet you and continue to exert their subtle influence on a less immediate level should testify to the natural qualities of materials and finishes. Real materials often benefit from being maintained in an equally natural way, with traditional oils, waxes and cleansers rather than synthetic wonder products that promise instant

results and leave the penetrating odour of ersatz pine, lemon or rose lingering in the air. Herbs planted in a sunny spot near the back door, freshly cut flowers, tomatoes ripening on a sill, something good to eat in the oven – these are hospitable, homely smells that do not come in a spray can.

If you focus on such basic elements, and take the lead from them, you are more likely to arrive at surroundings that express your personality and pleasures. What will be on view will reflect your tastes, your 'style' and not one you have imported from a television programme or the pages of a magazine.

Inevitably, on prominent view in many living areas there are computers, televisions and sound systems. Such technological intrusions can be strikingly at odds with the way the rest of a room looks: large black boxes and their accessories will quickly dominate the most sympathetic interior. Most of us, no matter how high-minded we pretend to be, are not going to forgo some form of in-house entertainment, but it is well worth looking for compact designs that blend in less obtrusively; with the miniaturization of technology, a small size represents no compromise in performance these days. While the television screen does need to be big enough for comfortable viewing, there are designs that are attractive enough not to be hidden away in cupboards: Philippe Starck's 'Jim Nature' television, in its recyclable casing, for example, introduces an element of tactility to this familiar piece of technology. Place the television so that it is in a good viewing position for the times you switch it on, but so that it is not occupying pride of place as a focal point. Perhaps if you have done your job properly and created a space that is truly relaxing, you will find yourself less inclined to switch on the box in the first place.

It goes without saying that however you choose to relax, it can only take place when the body is comfortable. Sitting or lounging on the floor can be very restful, but most of us in the West cannot maintain such postures for any length of time. This means that furniture design has a critical role to play.

Comfort may be hard to define, but most of us know it when we feel it, hence the popularity of bouncing on beds and sinking into sofas in furniture showrooms. Designers, however, have to start somewhere, and physical parameters begin to give shape to the idea. It is small wonder that chairs and sofas have arms, backs and legs just like we do. In a comfortable sofa, the angle or rake of the back answers the curvature of the spine, padding shields our bones from the rigid framework beneath, arms support our arms. We neither slump nor sit too upright. In an uncomfortable sofa, the hollow in the small of the back meets a vacancy, or the body slides forward to rest on the tailbone. Arms are high and dry, backs ache, breathing is constricted and we sink inevitably into a stupor.

The design process begins prosaically, with reference to anthropometric guidelines setting out basic human dimensions. Full-size sectional drawings are worked up on paper or screen; scale models add the third dimension, but for an assessment of comfort, there's no substitute for the real thing. It is just the same whether you are shopping for sofas or designing them – the final test is simply what it feels like. Whenever we design a sofa or armchair, or indeed any other product, the last stage before a design goes into production is the full-size sample. And there is no better way of assessing what changes must be made than inviting people of all shapes and sizes to come and try out the item in question. While certain parameters are common to us all and tiny variations – adjustments of a couple of degrees in the angle of the back, ten millimetres more on the width of the arms and the final choice of the fabric – can make all the difference, comfort has to be felt to be believed.

Shaped to fit the body, or padded and upholstered to provide a resilient seat for relaxation, the truly comfortable chair is a considerable design challenge.

touch

Cotton is exceptionally tough. The longest-staple fibres, such as Egyptian cotton, are strong enough to be woven into sailcloth. Line-drying may be time-consuming, but nothing smells better than sheets hung out in the sun and fresh air.

Touch offers creature comfort at its most basic and intimate. What we allow next to the skin – from the tips of the fingers to the soles of the feet – has an acute influence on the way we feel. The pleasure and reassurance we derive from such experiences starts at a young age. A baby nuzzles the satin binding on a 'security' blanket because it is a reminder of its mother's skin; a toddler clings to the familiar matted fur of a favourite teddy-bear; a child is hypersensitive to any clothing that is itchy or scratchy and inseparable from what is well worn and soft. Things that are nice to touch are frequently embedded with memories.

Touch can also be a performance-indicator: the honeycombed texture of waffleweave fabrics and the pile of terrycloth signal their superior absorbency; the dense weight of tightly woven wool suggests warmth.

One of the most delightful materials to touch is cashmere. Incredibly soft and featherlight, cashmere is spun from the exceptionally fine hairs of the cashmere goat, a species that lives in high, inaccessible parts of the world. The density and fineness of the animal's coat helps to trap a layer of warm air close to its skin and maintain body temperature in a cold mountain habitat. When the yarn is woven into blankets, shawls or clothing, the result is a material that provides an almost weightless warmth. Cashmere is costly, but unlike other more spurious forms of luxury, it is not expensive simply because it is expensive: there is a good reason for the price tag. Cashmere goats could be farmed in less remote areas that entail fewer transportation costs, but there would be little point – at lower altitudes there is no need for the goat to grow its fine, insulating undercoat. Spinning yarn from such delicate fibres is a relatively difficult process which also costs more than spinning sheep's wool, for example. Cashmere will never be cheap, but it is one of those luxuries that remain well worth the investment.

Cashmere can hardly be regarded as an essential, but many people could afford to be more discriminating in their choice of other fabrics and materials around the home. Most critical to comfort is the quality of bedlinen. While you may actually handle certain types of soft furnishings, such as curtains or tablecloths, only a couple of times a day, you spend nearly a third of your life lying between sheets or under a duvet. Bedlinen made of natural fibres may be more expensive than that made of synthetics and more difficult to wash and iron but the difference in price is negligible compared to the difference in comfort. Of course, people don't buy synthetic materials simply because they are cheaper but because they promise easy care. But if you compare the small amount of extra time you might need to spend maintaining bedlinen made of pure cotton or linen with the considerable degree of pleasure they offer during hours of use, the balance weighs firmly in their favour.

From the Middle Ages to the mechanization of cotton production, bedlinen, as the name suggests, was always made of linen, as were, for that matter, tablecloths, shirts and underclothes. Linen comes from the flax plant, grown widely in northern Europe; the fibre, which comes from the inner bark, is very strong, long-lasting and hard-wearing. Like all natural materials, the woven fabric has good 'transpirational' qualities, which means that it breathes. We experience this as a coolness and dryness on the skin – linen is quick to absorb moisture and quick to dry out. Old linen sheets are even better than new ones; the fabric simply grows softer with repeated washing. Linen is comparatively expensive, as processing flax is a complex procedure; the price is also determined by the basic characteristics of the fibre, with Belgium and Ireland producing the highest quality.

More affordable, but offering almost the same degree of tactile enjoyment, is pure cotton. Like linen, cotton has an ancient pedigree, dating back to early Egyptian, Indian and Chinese civilizations. It is now grown all over the world in warm to hot climatic zones, with a significant proportion of the world's output coming from the United States. As most of us appreciate from wearing cotton clothing, it is another fabric that breathes, allowing air to circulate next to the skin and making it a cool and comfortable material for both shirts and sheets.

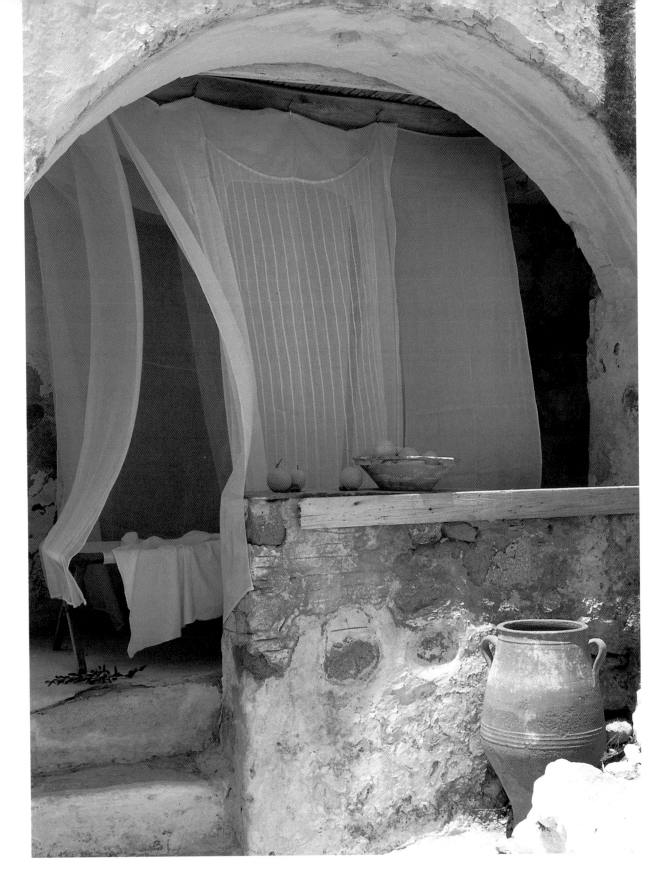

For those of us in northern latitudes, beds swathed in filmy drapery are purely romantic. In tropical areas, such a treatment has a practical purpose. Fine, light cotton, such as muslin, is often used as mosquito netting but it also allows air to circulate on hot, humid nights.

Textiles appeal to our sensual natures. Sumptuous fabrics such as velvet and brocade look and feel wonderful but, like leather, they can be overwhelming if used on a large scale. However, as accents – cushion covers, upholstery or throws – they bring an extra-special dimension of comfort.

Cotton is made from the fibres of the boll or fruit of the cotton plant. When the boll ripens and bursts, it frees seeds attached to fibrous tufts, tufts that are then harvested, dried, cleaned and pressed into bales for spinning. The quality of cotton is determined by the staple length, or length of the fibre. The highest quality cotton comes from long-staple fibres such as sea island and Egyptian, which can be woven into material light enough for the finest dress shirt or strong enough for the sails of a yacht. Short-staple cotton is grown mainly in Asia and results in coarser, less durable fabrics such as muslin, gingham and madras. Most cotton is woven from mid-range fibres; American cotton falls into this category. Perhaps genetic engineering will allow the staples to be lengthened.

Natural fibres, whether they are animal or vegetable in derivation, have built-in characteristics that help keep the body at an even temperature, neither too hot nor too cold. The same is true of other types of natural material used in the interior: stone floors in a hot climate or thick rugs in winter temper what would otherwise be extreme conditions and make them liveable. Synthetic products often fail spectacularly in this respect, as anyone who has spent a night sticking to or shivering between nylon sheets will testify. Feeling relaxed and easy in one's skin depends on the degree of basic comfort next to it.

On a more emotional level textiles, as one critic, Pamela Johnson of the University of East Anglia, has recently pointed out, can have a calming effect, related to the repetitive nature of the making process, whether it is weaving or knitting: 'The soothing process results in the soothing object.' Soothing is precisely the right term to describe the sensation of sliding between cool, clean cotton sheets or spreading a warm woollen blanket over your legs on a chilly night. Smoothness is also soothing – we are instinctively drawn to surfaces as soft as skin.

Fabrics can arouse passionate responses. One of those who admires the quality of different materials is Min Hogg, editor of *The World of Interiors*, who believes that fabrics epitomize 'everything that is glorious about man's ability to make something', expressing the disciplines of different techniques from industrial engineering to handmaking. Nothing gives her more pleasure than the noises fabrics make, how they feel when you touch them or the way that light falls on a crumpled piece of taffeta, for example. Just as clean sheets offer a 'frisson of pleasure', she recommends that all covers and curtains be machine-washable.

I began my career as a textile designer and in a book I once wrote about the subject I said, 'Pattern fulfils two human needs in that it can be both stimulating and tranquillizing.' For 'pattern' I could have equally substituted 'texture'; in the context

We are most aware of comfort next to the skin, which means that our choice of bedlinen is critical. Natural fabrics, such as cotton, linen and wool, feel and perform infinitely better than their synthetic counterparts, and are well worth the extra investment of time and money. Whether you are a devotee of the duvet or a sheet-and-blankets fan, quality matters. Immaculate detailing, such as button fastenings, adds finesse.

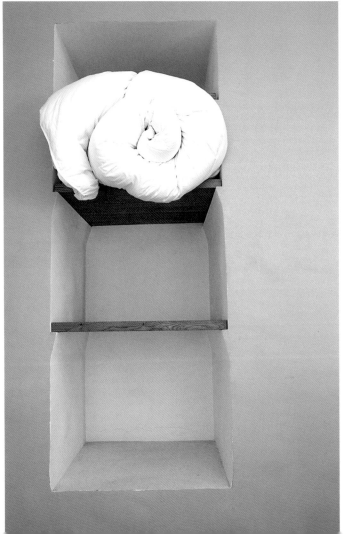

of textiles such elements are often interchangeable. Any textile designer must understand how cloth is woven and this is all the more important where patterns are woven in, rather than printed on, the surface. When we design a new range of bedlinen, for example, the process may begin on paper, but, as is the case with the prototype sofa, a key stage is translating a two-dimensional idea into something approximating the real thing. For a fabric designed to be woven in stripes of colour, this stage might consist of making 'windings' where the pattern of colours is translated into alternating yarns or threads wound round a strip of foam board or card. This part of the design process supplies the dimension missing from the drawing board – that of touch.

As the terms bedclothes and bedlinen indicate, there is a close relationship between the materials we wear and those with which we dress the home, which may account for the affection they inspire. Sofa and chair upholstery can be clean-lined and tailored or loose and unstructured, while such details as cushion covers could be seen as the fashionable accessory of the home's wardrobe, supplying an accent of colour or contrast of texture that brings a look together. The clothing metaphor can be taken almost literally: knitted cushion covers fastened with horn buttons are only one step removed from the woolly jumper in your drawer. A dévoré velvet throw is merely a bigger example of what you might wrap round your shoulders. Suede trousers and suede cushions appear in the shops at the same time, sharing the same fashionable cachet. We would probably feel overwhelmed by such materials if they were used on a much larger scale – suede or velvet covering every chair, bed and window would be sheer overkill unless you were designing a bordello – but as small 'touches' they add a sense of vitality and perhaps a hint of eroticism.

As far as touch is concerned, the surface that offers potentially the highest degree of daily contact is the floor. We walk on it, sit on it, lounge on it; it is the first surface we meet when we get out of bed or the bath; children crawl and play on it. Even with the protection of shoes, the floor can provide a textural dimension, an interest that is further developed

The way different fabrics feel
can indicate how they will
perform practically. The thick
pile of terrycloth soaks up
moisture from the skin; similarly,
the indentations in waffleweave
are what make it so absorbent.
Steer clear of poor quality towels
– they may feel dense and heavy
when you buy them, but many
have added bulking agents that
vanish at the first wash.

when different materials are combined: brick and wood, stone and rug, slate and marble. But the visual delight offered by textural variety is not the same as the pleasure of touch. Flooring made of natural plant fibres, such as sisal, coir and seagrass, appear full of character when you look at them, but can be distinctly lacking in comfort: all you have to do is ask a child. However, in eastern cultures, such as that of Japan, where shoelessness is the norm indoors, and living traditionally takes place at floor level, more attention is paid to comfort underfoot. The springiness of smooth tatami matting made from fine reeds is both resilient enough to sit on and sleep on and kind to stockinged feet.

Walking barefoot or in stockinged feet is one of the most relaxing things you can do. Although we may keep our shoes on for most of the time in the West, it is certainly worth providing something enjoyable and accommodating to step on, at least in those areas where encounters between bare feet and floor take place regularly. Carpet or a rug by the side of the bed, cork or slatted wooden mats by the bath, mosaic tiles in the shower stall and worn flagstones on a sunny terrace give pleasure from the ground up.

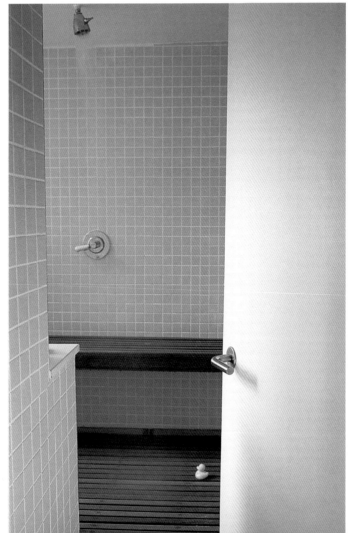

Touch connects us with the physical world. Natural materials provide a variety of tactile experiences that give pleasure on a barely conscious level but which are no less important for that. The feel of cotton or linen next to the skin, or smooth stone, mosaic or wood underfoot cannot be simulated.

sleep

Marilyn Monroe famously wore only Chanel No 5 in hers, but even if you are less minimally dressed between the sheets, bed is still the place where we are most critically aware of comfort or the lack of it. The fairy tale about the princess who was so sensitive that she could detect the presence of a single pea lurking under layers and layers of feather bedding is generally read as a parable about gentility and refinement, but it could serve equally well as an illustration of how even minor shortfalls in bedroom comfort can make for nights of troubled sleep.

Sleep deprivation, as any new parent or torturer worth his salt could tell you, is the fastest route to mental and physical collapse. The body needs sleep to replenish its energy reserves, to fight off illness and to rest muscles and joints; arguably, we also need sleep to dream, the activity during which the mind beds down the experiences of the day. A sleepless night (what the French call *une nuit blanche*, or 'a white night') often precedes a disastrous day beset by accidents, lapses in concentration and bad temper; after a good night's sleep, most people are ready, both physically and mentally, for anything. Sleep is much more than the ultimate in relaxation.

Many things can keep you awake at night – noisy neighbours, crying babies, snoring partners, looming deadlines, unresolved problems – but there is no reason why your bed should be one of them. A decent bed is the bottom line in night-time comfort and the most important purchase you will ever make. A good bed can certainly be stylish, but there is absolutely no point in forking out huge sums on a four-poster with all the fancy trimmings if the mattress is substandard or the bed base is flimsy. The quality of a bed rests in more prosaic details of construction and composition which are rarely apparent at first sight but should be immediately obvious the minute you lie down.

If one should always try to buy the best that one can afford, this is doubly true when it comes to choosing a bed. A good bed – specifically, a good mattress – supports the body's weight, cushions the spine and is resilient enough to accommodate shifts of position without sagging.

Comfort makes the difference between sweet dreams and a restless night. The best bed and mattress you can afford are essential for healthy sleep and daily well-being.

People have varying tastes when it comes to the softness or hardness of beds, but in practical terms the spectrum is actually fairly narrow. If the mattress is too hard and unyielding, the body will be forced out of its natural alignment; if it is too soft, your weight will simply trap you in a fixed position for the entire night. The result, in either case, will be cramp, stiff joints and sore muscles or, worse, long-term back problems. Factor another person who may be a different height, a different weight and have a different sleeping pattern into the equation and the demands become more acute. A good mattress should not be a seesaw, always tipping down on the side bearing the most weight. It should also be covered in a durable material made of natural fibre, such as cotton ticking, to allow air to circulate and promote the absorption of moisture.

The quality of a mattress is determined primarily by the method of construction. The best and most expensive mattresses are made up of a large number of individual springs set into pockets. As the springs move independently, the mattress will give only where weight is applied, providing the optimum comfort for two people sharing a bed, especially desirable where the weights differ greatly. Another type of sprung mattress consists of a continuous network or coil of springs; the denser the springs, the better the quality. Solid foam mattresses, which are specifically designed to be used with sprung bases, also vary in thickness, comfort and, hence, quality.

When it comes to sleeping habits, people generally fall into two categories: larks and owls. But even if you like to sleep late in a darkened room, windows are essential to allow fresh air to circulate. In Britain, at least, a room is not deemed 'habitable' unless it has a window. Shutters screen the light almost totally (far left), **while placing the bed so that the light falls at the foot of it rather than at the top prevents early morning glare** (left). **A wrap-around view of sea and sky would appeal to true early birds** (below).

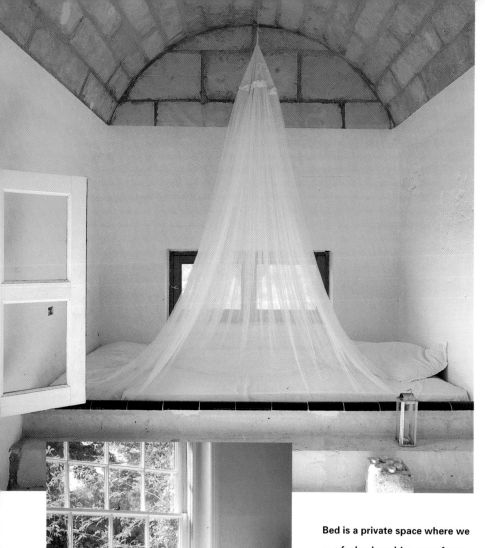

Pillows also vary in content and quality; choose the variety that provides the best support for your neck and head. Down-filled pillows are the most expensive and softest; more resilient are feather-and-down mixtures or all-feather. Goose and duck feathers are naturally curly, giving added springiness. Synthetic fibre or foam pillows are advisable if you suffer from allergies.

Unfortunately, unlike other purchases made with an eye for quality, mattresses do not improve with time. Regular turning, from side to side and top to bottom, will help to distribute wear evenly, and regular airing is essential, but all mattresses have a finite lifespan, normally no longer than about a decade. Pillows last a much shorter time; when they become floppy and saggy, it's time for them to go.

What we sleep between is just as important as what we sleep on. As I have mentioned earlier, sheets and bedding made of natural fibres create a temperate zone next to the skin, a soothing combination of dryness, coolness and smoothness. But the body also needs warmth, which is where the duvet versus blankets debate comes in. I can take some credit for introducing the duvet to British households; we first stocked 'continental quilts' in Habitat in 1964. Since that time, the majority in this country have overcome their initial suspicions and woken up to the duvet's

Bed is a private space where we can feel vulnerable; some form of enclosure, or suggestion of it, makes us feel more secure. Even in cool climates, simple drapery such as suspended netting can be very atmospheric (above). **Sunlight streams over this bed placed snugly against a window reveal** (left). **In a high-ceilinged space, the position of the bed by the staircase creates a feeling of intimacy** (right). **One of the most appealing sleeping arrangements is the box bed** (far right)**; tongue-and-groove panelling and a useful ledge makes a cosy alcove.**

The trusses, beams and columns of this converted attic create natural points of demarcation between different areas.

considerable practical advantages. Warm, light and obviating the need for time-consuming bedmaking, the duvet has now all but lost the 'foreignness' of its origins to become an unremarkable household basic. Available in different densities or 'tog' ratings for varying degrees of warmth, the best duvets owe their superb insulating characteristics to real feathers and/or down rather than synthetic fibres. Tastes are notoriously fickle, however, and along with the ubiquity of the duvet has come a renewed affection for old-fashioned sheets and blankets among the fashion-conscious or those lucky enough to have somebody to make the bed for them – this is perhaps the result of perceived, rather than actual, comfort.

Bed, however, is more than a comfortable place to sleep. As the duvet/blanket divide reveals, a certain sense of nostalgia can have more than a part to play. Bed is the ultimate personal domain; in fact, it is our first private space. The attachment most children feel to their own beds, despite their disinclination to go to sleep, is profoundly territorial and this sense of refuge or nesting instinct lingers on into adulthood. Whether we huddle under the duvet, or draw up the blankets, bed offers psychological and emotional comfort as well as the merely physical. This may be why eating in bed, reading in bed, thinking in bed and even working in bed can seem such pleasant indulgences.

This broader dimension of comfort can be enhanced – or undermined – by the way you arrange, furnish and light the bedroom. The bedroom, which, like the bathroom, is defined by its dominant piece of furniture, tends to persist even in the most determinedly open-plan living spaces. Enclosure and physical separation from other activities not only provide the privacy we desire for intimate moments, but also offer a sense of security when we feel at our most vulnerable.

Where you place the bed is a critical factor. Feng shui, as ever, has an answer for this, which is that the bed should be placed with the head against a wall to ensure solidity, stability and security, and facing the door or entrance but not directly lined up with it (in feng shui terms, a bed directly facing an open doorway is little better than a coffin ready to be carted down the stairs). More prosaically, it makes sense to position the bed so that there is plenty of clear space surrounding it, to avoid the low-level frustration that results when bedmaking becomes an obstacle course and to give each side of the bed equal ease of access.

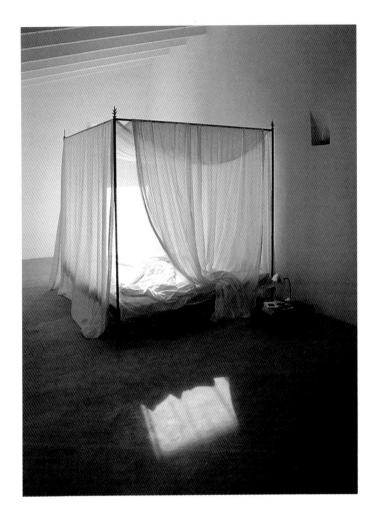

We no longer need heavy bed drapery to provide warmth, but even light fabric can offer a sense of enclosure.

Naturally, feng shui also has a great deal to say on the subject of orientation, that is which point of the compass the bed should face. South is recommended for fame, north for success in business, east for a happy family life, and so on. (It's not clear what you should do if you want to achieve all these aims – place the bed on a revolving pedestal, perhaps.) We might find the issue of orientation more relevant in terms of the quality of light. A room facing east, for example, catches the early morning sun; dawn light provides a gentler and more natural way of waking up than a buzzing alarm clock.

Light control is much more important in bedrooms than might first be imagined, given that a large proportion of the time we spend there is during the hours of darkness. In urban areas, however, the spill of light from streetlamps means that darkness is rarely total, and some form of screening is essential. On the other hand, morning light creates an inherent mood of optimism, so a complete blackout is usually

a bad idea. Curtains or blinds that filter the light rather than block it out entirely strike a balance. As far as artificial lighting is concerned, it is crucial to avoid overhead glare from a central fixture; if such an arrangement is harsh in a living area, it is twice as uncomfortable when your principal viewpoint is from a supine position. In a similar way, bedrooms benefit from good ventilation; fresh air is just as important as the right lighting in creating revitalizing and restful conditions. Deadening sound can also be an important consideration, especially if you live in a busy urban area, but even a cock crowing in the country can wake you earlier than you wish.

A comfortable bed, subtle light and gentle airflow provide the basic ingredients for peaceful sleep – and for those key transitory times when we unwind and wake up. But the bedroom, despite its name, often gathers in a variety of other functions and their accompanying paraphernalia – activities that can erode the contemplative mood.

Le Corbusier, who we have to remember was Swiss, had strong opinions on this subject as on many others; he is well known for denouncing the habit of keeping clothes in the bedroom, a practice he regarded as unsanitary. His view may display a rather zealous attitude to personal hygiene but it does hint at the potential for conflict. While I doubt that dressing in the bedroom poses a significant risk to one's health, it does entail turning a large portion of the available space over to storage. Traditional pieces of storage furniture, such as wardrobes and chests of drawers, devour space and serve as additional navigational obstacles in a room where the bed already takes up a considerable amount of floor area. Open storage systems, such as clothes rails and fitted shelving may be physically less intrusive but the overall effect can be rather like sleeping in a shop. If you are going to share your sleeping space with your entire wardrobe, it makes sense to construct closets and other concealed forms of storage that provide an uninterrupted background. Better still, borrow space from somewhere else – a landing, bathroom or hallway – and build a dressing area where you can organize your clothes systematically.

Min Hogg has recently put one of her 'room theories' into practice, turning what had formerly been, at various times, a dining room and a spare room into a dressing room. What might at first seem a dramatic, almost wilful, sacrifice of space has had an entirely beneficial effect: the change it has made to her life is 'a joy', she says. Her clothes, bags, shoes and scarves are still housed all in one place, but she can now shut the door on them, and if they become disorganized, it takes only a matter of seconds to get them back into what she considers to be good order. However, the greatest advantage she has discovered is that by moving her 'clutter and clobber' elsewhere, the bedroom has been released into a more 'living' room.

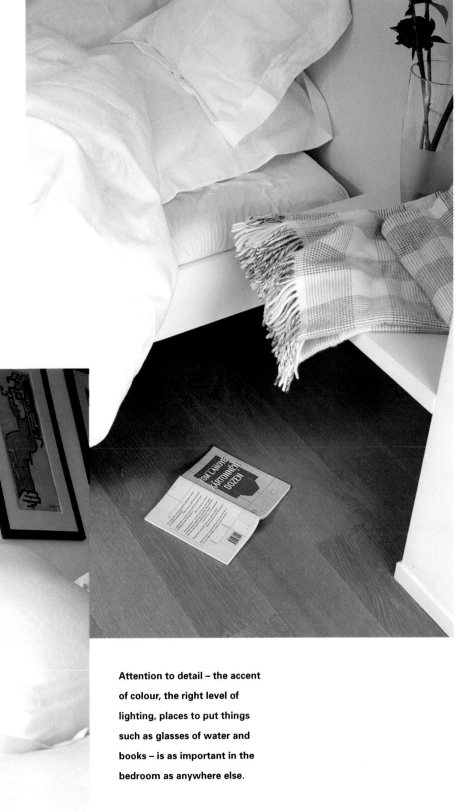

Attention to detail – the accent of colour, the right level of lighting, places to put things such as glasses of water and books – is as important in the bedroom as anywhere else.

bathe

Water is undoubtedly therapeutic, the directness of contact being part of the pleasure. This minimal shower (far right), designed by Claudio Silvestrin, is little more than a water jet set into a panel of stone, which reduces bathing to the bare essentials.

Bathing, for all its virtuous connotations, is less about function than pleasure and comfort. Few of us nowadays, in our machine-washed, dry-cleaned clothes and white-collar jobs, get as visibly dirty as we would have done in previous centuries working on the land or at some other form of heavy manual labour. Just as the advent of domestic appliances, such as the vacuum cleaner, increased our expectations of how clean a home could be, indoor plumbing, dependable drainage and endless hot water have extended our standards of personal hygiene. It has never been easier to keep clean, but scrubbing off the grime of a hard day's toil at a computer terminal must realistically rank second in importance to the sheer sensual bliss of a hot soak or the mental invigoration of a shower. Today, most of us bathe primarily to wash away our cares; keeping clean goes without saying.

Water has a powerful appeal. From sea-bathing to skinny-dipping or simply messing around in boats, it provides a focus for countless holidays. You might trace the fascination to our ancestors' supposed origins in the primeval oceans, or no further back than the womb, but water is a medium that feels both instinctively pleasurable and utterly therapeutic.

It is odd, then, when we have regularly gone to considerable lengths to seek out spas, seasides and water resorts, that the bathroom, which offers immediate access to similarly elemental delights, has often been one of the least satisfactory areas in the home. Until fairly recently, cold, clinical and cramped would have been a fair description of many British bathrooms, the meanness of the aesthetic reflecting, perhaps, a coyness about bodily functions, coupled with a certain puritanical suspicion of well-being – not surprising, I suppose, in a race brought up to believe in the moral value of the cold shower. There are, however, encouraging signs that a certain reassessment is underway. The change in attitude, like many shifts in the way we view our homes, has gone hand in hand with an increased exposure to the wider world.

I can vividly remember the experience of bathing in a hotel in the Italian resort of Positano. The bathroom window looked out over the sea, which was pleasant enough, but the lower portion of the window was fashioned into a glazed fish tank. From one's eyeline, then, sitting in the tub, there was this incredibly watery view, with the fish in the tank merging almost seamlessly with the blue sea beyond. In terms of capturing the mood of the setting, the effect far surpassed the desultory collection of seashells or display of beachcombing relics that seem to be the more typical expressions of seaside inspiration.

That experience was unique and specific. Other inspirational influences may come from contact with the bathing customs of different cultures. The Scandinavian sauna, Turkish steam bath, Japanese jacuzzi or Californian hot tub display very different approaches to relaxing and/or keeping clean, but their common denominator is a certain uninhibited, if not to say communal, enjoyment of water, steam or heat. Although it is not necessary and, indeed, for many people it may be prohibitively expensive or impractical to install the required fixtures and fittings in the home, the basic attitude is well worth emulating.

The pleasures of bathing are enhanced when the setting provides a link with the outside world. In a warm climate, fresh breezes through open doorways and a tantalizing garden view are the next best thing to showering outdoors – and the antithesis of a cramped cell-like space with its punitive overtones.

The first step, surely, must be to create surroundings that are pleasant to spend time in. The challenge is to do so within very real, practical constraints. The clinical bathroom, with its tetchy undercurrent of anxiety about germs and smells, is often a repellent place where no one would wish to linger, but its laboratory-style functionalism is at least easy to maintain in a pristine state. At the opposite extreme, bathrooms furnished and fitted rather like shrunken drawing rooms are ultimately intolerant of the activities that must take place there: sodden carpet, persistent odours, mildew and damp-stained walls do not add up to an easy environment. And dressed-up, formal bathrooms can seem rather peculiar surroundings for an activity that requires you to be naked.

Somewhere between these two extremes are bathrooms whose design is founded on the display of a sympathetic mix of materials. Combinations of stone, mosaic, ceramics, glass, metal or tongue-and-groove boarding perform well on a functional level and invite our continuing interest in their evocative textural contrasts, an interest that is only heightened in a state of undress. Bathrooms where materials speak for themselves offer a way of getting back to basics – surely one of the main attractions of bathing.

As far as planning is concerned, be as generous with space as you can: think of the delightfully pampering quality of a bathroom in a good hotel. A big bathroom and a big bath lift the spirits and liberate the mind for creative daydreaming, which is another one of the pleasures of bathing. Equally important, a larger area permits flexibility of layout, so the bath can be positioned in a freer arrangement, either with just its head against the wall or pulled away from the wall entirely and aligned to take advantage of a view. A greater degree of space allows a more congenial segregation of activities than a confined bathroom, which can often be fitted out in only one way, with lavatory, bath and washbasin in a tight grouping that is as constricting physically as it is psychologically. A big bathroom also means that there is space in between these necessary fixtures for other pieces of furniture, such as chests, chairs or free-standing shelves, which can make a bathroom so hospitable. But if your spatial

If the bathroom is spacious, it can often be a good idea to position the bath tub so that it projects out from the wall, leaving free space on three sides. Views are equally important, as are windows that open to admit light and air, even a patch of warming sunshine.

options are very limited, remember that even a small amount of extra floor area can make a difference when it comes to juggling the planning. A doorway pulled out into a hallway by a matter of inches can give you just enough extra elbow room at a basin, for example, to make the layout workable.

'Sanitaryware', that unlovely trade term, sums up the whole no-nonsense style of standardized bathroom fittings, whose basic form has altered very little in the century or so since the demise of Thomas Crapper, the Victorian Emperor of the Bog. There's nothing wrong with such fittings, provided they are of decent quality and size – and, of course, provided they are white – but aesthetically they offer little more than the comfort of the expected. More recently, new designs have emerged that take a more playful, sculptural approach to the whole issue. Cantilevered basins in glass or metal, sinks that defiantly expose the working plumbing, tubs that are sleek and streamlined or big-bellied and free-standing run the full stylistic gamut from minimal to expressive, while at the technological cutting edge, showers or taps lit fibre-optically turn running water into a theatrical play of light; there are even Japanese lavatories that wash your bottom with warm water and dry it with jets of air. An unusual location can be enough to create a provocative sense of surprise – a bath sunk flush with the floor, for example.

One of the most luxurious bathrooms in fiction is described in F. Scott Fitzgerald's story 'The Diamond As Big As The Ritz'. It, too, features a sunken bath, into which the main character, John T. Unger, is propelled by a tilting bed via a fleecy incline into an adjoining bath chamber: '. . . lining the walls of the room and the sides and bottom of the bath itself was a blue aquarium, and gazing through the crystal surface on which he sat, he could see fish swimming among amber lights and even gliding without curiosity past his outstretched toes . . . .' The sensual ambience is heightened by fountains that disperse hot rosewater, paddle-wheels that churn up a frothy foam, a 'moving-picture machine' and ambient flutes 'dripping a melody that was like a waterfall'. Unger's bath ends with a cold salt-water shower and a massage with 'oil, alcohol and spice'.

The luxury of this imagined bathtime rests in having everything done for you. A slightly more practical solution was designed by Le Corbusier for the family of some friends

Wet skin loses heat rapidly; thick, generous towels and mats to soak up the moisture are a vital part of bathroom comfort.

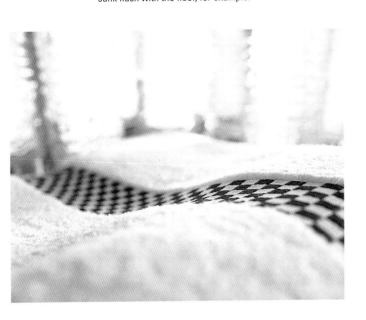

The water chute at Ahmadabad, India, designed by Le Corbusier, connects the summer sleeping platform on the roof of the house to the garden pool (preceding pages).

of mine at Ahmadabad in India. He had been commissioned by the parents to build a house and asked the two boys how they dreamed they might bathe in the morning. They said they would like to roll out of bed into a large, cool pool. Corbusier's solution was to construct a long terrazzo slide, lubricated with the constant trickle of water, running from the summer sleeping platform on the roof into the pool in the garden below. It is the perfect way to begin the day in the heat of India.

In Philippe Starck's recent bathroom designs, based on the archetypal container shapes of the bucket and trough, the aim is neither to overturn convention nor induce a sense of pampered luxury. Instead, it is to reacquaint us with a directness of experience and remind us of those simple acts such as stooping down to cup water from a pool or pouring a jug of water over one's body – similar to those unsophisticated, unselfconscious moments of intimacy seen in the paintings of Degas and Bonnard. The basic premise is, perhaps, that plumbing, by delivering water on tap, has somehow managed to distance us from the true feeling of spontaneity that bathing can offer.

As with sleeping, bathing is an activity where comfort is as critical before and after it takes place as it is during the event. Towels or robes warmed on a heated rail, non-slip surfaces underfoot, generous towels to absorb water from your body are just as integral to a comfortable bath as the right water temperature. Wet skin quickly becomes cold and is more susceptible to abrasion from rough textures, which is why the quality of bath towels and flannels is important. Terrycloth is not as absorbent as commonly supposed, especially if it has been given a velvet finish;

A bathroom in a converted Brussels shop offers a charming departure from the expected (above)**: the sink plumbed into an old free-standing cupboard, metal boxes and trunks for storage and a claw-foot bath.**

Many bathrooms and cloakrooms are necessarily small; a wall covered in mirror multiplies the sense of space (right). **A room with a view: this low-level bath sunk into the floor and screened by blinds and curtains is the perfect spot for daydreaming** (below).

waffleweave fabrics soak up water much more readily. Cheap towels, even those that give every impression of softness, have often been treated with chemicals to improve the way they feel, a temporary finish that can increase water-resistance. After a few washes, however, a poor quality product will be all too obvious.

The bathroom has traditionally been the focus for much spurious luxury, with coloured suites, mahogany loo seats, gilt taps and ostentatious brass-plated shower sets. At the same time, the Victorian notion of 'cleanliness is next to godliness' has taken quite a mystic turn during recent years, with bathside candles and aromatherapy oils elevating the entire bathing experience to a kind of high communion. I'm all for the sybaritic pleasures of fine soaps and scents but, for me, the real luxury of bathing remains its easy simplicity.

function

Easy living demands a home that works as well as it looks. Things that function properly and suit the task for which they are required, a basic infrastructure that is accommodating and well planned, and a natural sense of order smooth your path. Easy living, of course, could mean getting someone else to do all the work for you, but as a person who actually enjoys what he does, I prefer to think of it as a way of ensuring that work itself is a pleasure.

Splitting life down the middle, with chores in one half and fun in the other, seems profoundly unsatisfactory to me. Real pleasure goes hand in hand with practicality: a kitchen that is functional will also be a place of creative satisfaction; knives, forks and glasses that perform the way they should and look good will add joy to the experience of eating and drinking. Drudgery – which we're all keen to avoid – is not merely monotonous physical effort but a relentless uphill struggle where things are constantly breaking, failing or getting lost and materials are just not up to scratch.

Throughout this century, mechanization has been seen as the universal answer to the problem of work. But turning to technology as a fail-safe way of making life easier can be a Faustian pact. Everyone is familiar with the household gadget that takes longer to find, assemble, operate, clean and put away again than the procedure it is designed to perform. Such 'labour-saving' devices only save labour in the narrowest sense when the button is pressed or switch is flicked; in the wider scheme of things they can be irritating, time-consuming and difficult to use and maintain. Of course, I am not suggesting that one should turn the clock back, replace vacuum cleaners with carpet beaters or scrub the sheets by hand, but there are many situations when a simple, direct approach remains the easiest and most enjoyable of all. A good, sharp knife, for example, functions far more efficiently in ordinary circumstances than the most heavily accessorized food processor, and when it 'fails', you simply have to sharpen it, not reread the instruction manual, hunt for the lost part, check the guarantee or phone the supplier – only to be told that the model is now out of production and cannot be repaired.

Technology, which is supposed to be our helpmate, can often leave us helpless. An amusing story recently appeared in the papers about Bill Gates' first night in his new 'smart' house. A large television screen, programmed to slide in and out of a console on demand, refused either to retract or turn off. Unfortunately, the screen was located in the bedroom and, in the interests of a decent night's sleep, the only solution was to throw a blanket over it. No doubt we will be throwing blankets over many technological gizmos on 1st January 2000, at one minute past midnight.

Anyone who has ever been driven into a blind fury by a non-functioning piece of equipment whose breakdown is as total as it is mysterious will recognize the frustration. My own central heating system is so intelligent that when it goes wrong I have no access to it or way of coping with it; my only recourse is to ring the service engineers. Such situations bring to mind a comment once made by the president of the French booksellers' association. Faced with the failure of a complex audiovisual presentation, he reminded those of us in the audience that 'books don't break'. In this sense,

technology can also be distancing, replacing a directness of experience and control with something that requires the expert intervention of third parties. It seems to me that one of the components of an easy life is to surround yourself only with well-proven technology; the cutting edge can damage your life.

Rather than investing in technology that will end up running the show or dominating all your waking hours, I believe it is better to spend time thinking about what you really need and the way you like to live. On one level, everyone needs the basic degree of practicality where services are well integrated, pipes and wires are hidden, controls are properly positioned and taps do not drip or leak. But on another level, what makes your home function properly and your life easier may be very different from the type of surroundings that work for others. Min Hogg, for example, insists on keeping a pair of scissors in every room, despite the fact that she lives in an apartment and not a rambling house on several levels. For others, it may be always having pen and paper close to hand or never being far from a socket for plugging in the laptop computer . . . easy living rests on the fundamental principle of suiting yourself.

order

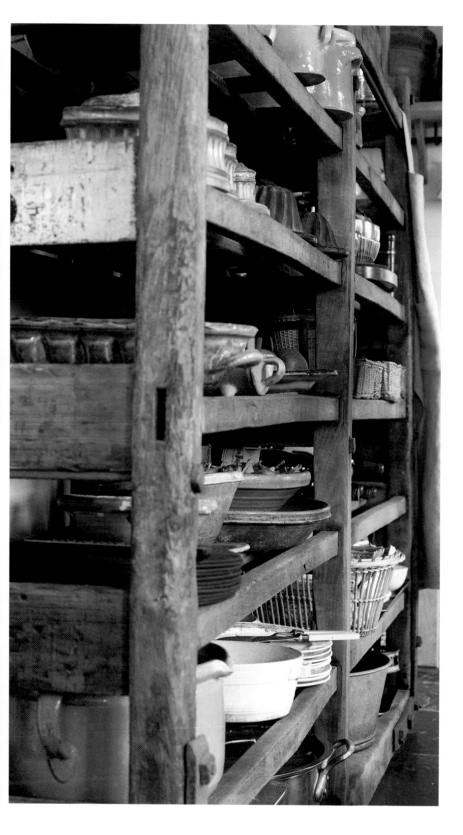

The principle is the same, although the aesthetic is different. Storage basically consists of variations on very simple themes: shelving, hanging and containing.

Life attracts clutter as surely as a letterbox attracts junk mail. You may begin with a relatively clean slate but within a terrifying short space of time find yourself sharing your home with a morass of irrelevant detail: gadgets you never use, instruction manuals for gadgets you no longer own, unwelcome gifts and wedding presents, clothes that don't fit or suit you, spare parts for machines you have long since upgraded, half-consumed packets of foodstuffs you don't like, books that don't bear a second reading and, worse, books that, if you are honest with yourself, you are never going to read in the first place.

It is not particularly difficult to identify what is redundant baggage, nor is it hard to get rid of it. In many cases, all it takes is a little ruthlessness and a few spare moments; at the most painful, you should need only the relatively small degree of courage that is required to look the bad bargain or false economy straight in the eye and discard it, sadder but certainly wiser.

On this level, good order is merely common sense. Time is one of the most valuable commodities we have and if you are one of those people who seems to spend ninety per cent of their waking hours looking for things, sparing an hour or two for a clearout is the single most important step you can take towards improving your life. Clutter in this sense is simply a waste of energy, where ordinary routines are unnecessarily complicated, and there is the constant feeling of working in your own shadow. Clutter can also be expensive: plenty of people who regularly find themselves turning the house upside down looking for some essential tool or ingredient wind up buying another in sheer desperation.

But, as most people soon come to realize, the whole issue is not quite as simple as that. Personal taste also plays a part. Some people, myself included, are incredibly refreshed by simplicity – whether a clear desk, a clear floor or the sense of spaciousness and expansion that results when every available surface is not weighted down with its own cargo of belongings. Others seem to need their possessions more visibly around them, within easy, familiar reach. The expression of such nesting instincts, although they may result in environments that would cause a minimalist to recoil with horror, constitutes a very real part of what gives some of us pleasure in our own surroundings.

While I naturally subscribe to the 'fewer and better' school of thinking, I would hate everything to be under rigid control, regimented behind the closed doors of seamlessly built-in cupboards. It isn't easy living when you daren't leave newspapers strewn across the floor or an open book by the bedside: in such uptight interiors, living itself seems an intrusion. I might enjoy the uplifting sight of a clear desk, but I also take a certain pleasure from the creative messiness that is the natural by-product of work. Francis Bacon worked in the untidiest space imaginable, but produced some of the finest paintings of the twentieth century.

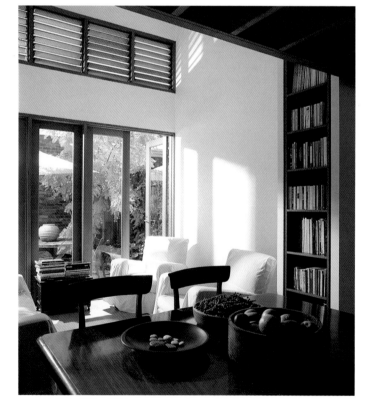

If order is to some extent in the eye of the beholder, occupying a variable position somewhere in the long continuum between minimalism and chaos, it also requires daily compromise in most households. Just as there are couples where one partner is always early and the other always late, the person who always knows where the scissors are often finds themselves sharing their life with someone who hasn't seen the bottom of their sock drawer since 1987. From the two-year-old's continual emptying of drawers, cupboards and toy boxes in the spirit of playful enquiry, to the unrivalled squalor of the teenage bedroom, children are a different matter entirely.

Living with someone who has diametrically opposed views on order can be far from easy, but it is nevertheless a challenge most of us can manage to meet. Joseph, for example, is more of a minimalist than his wife Isabel, who likes a softer look. He believes, however, that 'it is important to bring the personalities of two people together'. Suzie Slesin, on the other hand, is a self-confessed accumulator, whose work as a magazine design editor and author of numerous

Tolerance for clutter varies widely from person to person. For those who prefer very little on view, discreet storage is particularly important. In this clutter-free zone (above left)**, cupboards built into a low-level plinth provide efficient stowing places for everyday belongings. Storage that forms an integral part of the architecture of a space can be particularly satisfying. Shelves fitted around a door or within a tall alcove** (above and left) **read as a structural element, not as an afterthought. Ron Arad's 'Bookworm'** (right) **turns storage into something altogether more playful and sculptural.**

books on style presents her with many opportunities to travel and acquire the objects of her current passions. Inevitably, her husband would prefer to live with the bare minimum. Pressure of space in their New York apartment has meant that he has had to forgo his dream of a separate clothes closet; in turn, she has stopped going to flea markets and is in what she calls a 'deacquisition phase'. Her dilemma, common to everybody who loves and is inspired by things, is that the more you buy or collect, the less space you have left to appreciate them.

It is a dilemma I have felt myself. In the living room of my house in the country, I have tried to resolve this by displaying lots of things that please me at one end of the room but keeping the other end relatively empty, so you can sit in one half and look at the other without feeling overwhelmed by clutter. Joseph, who is equally beguiled by possessions, has learned 'to appreciate things in other places rather than mine'. With communications so advanced and with so many images in books and magazines, he believes that 'it is silly to try to have everything one likes'.

What is even more important than working out a compromise is recognizing what your own tastes are in the first place. In Suzie Slesin's view, accepting who you are and what you like is the basis for easy living. 'I would love to have a plain, empty bedroom,' she says, 'but when I'm in bed I like to have a stack of magazines and books nearby and I like to be able to see photographs of my children. That means I have to provide a place to put these things.' Knowing how you like to live is fundamental to creating a home that has a truly workable sense of order, which is, after all, the only sort that counts.

Given our varying attitudes to clutter and order, there are nevertheless some strategies everyone can profit by. The first, as already discussed, is to get rid of what is redundant and meaningless. You may like a lot of things around you, but there is no good reason why such items should be ugly, useless or past their sell-by date. The second is to provide sensible homes for what you do decide to keep. There is a real pleasure in what Min Hogg calls 'stowing', finding good practical places to keep things. Even children, for all their chaotic disorganization, instinctively appreciate the appeal of squirrelling things away. The childhood 'treasure' box, filled with arcane collections of meaningful bits and pieces is essentially, as one critic has said, a 'portable, tangible secret'. The pleasure of stowing owes something to this feeling, as well as the sense of resourcefulness that comes when cupboards are well stocked and shipshape.

Storage conceived as part of the overall visual effect of the room and designed to fit what is being stored is profoundly satisfying. In Min's case, two sides of her kitchen are fitted with shelves at the upper level – a narrow one for glasses so that they can be arranged only two deep, and a wider one that takes plates, stacked one pile deep. The array of glasses and plates forms an intrinsic part of the room's look.

Equally important, however, is that everything is accessible and nothing is shoved to the back of a cupboard where it won't be noticed or get used. Accessibility, in its wider sense, also means arranging your possessions so that you take some account of how often you will need them. Daily use means right at hand; once a year at Christmas means stored out of the way in the loft.

Some of the most appealing 'stowing' places are storage rooms. The dressing room, larder, workshop, shed or garage, with belongings neatly organized and in one place, may initially seem like a sacrifice of space, but can vastly improve the way that surrounding living areas work. Similarly, wide hallways lined with bookshelves or cupboards can be both extremely hard-working and full of architectural character. I particularly enjoy the ingenuity of small fitted spaces: the lockers of a ship's cabin or the detailing of old Pullman coaches on trains can be an inspiration for home storage.

All types of storage consist of variations on very simple themes: containing (in cupboards, drawers, baskets or boxes), hanging (from rails, racks, pegs or hooks) or shelving. Such basic formats have an inherent versatility, which is part of their appeal and their practicality. A wire-mesh trolley, for example, could provide storage for home office supplies, cosmetics, toys or vegetables. In the same way, the borrowing of storage fittings and furniture from retail and commercial sectors is an expression of their inherent flexibility as much as an appreciation of their looks.

Storage can be less satisfactory, however, when it involves specific accessories, such as plastic pocketed shoe 'tidies' or drawer inserts for segregating every pair of pants or socks. Such forms of organization can be irritating and fiddly to use; rather than streamlining your belongings, they simply introduce another level of clutter. A classic example of this appeared recently in a mail-order catalogue in the form of a 'stair basket'. This shaped wicker container was designed to provide a home for all those items that collect at the bottom of the stairs, awaiting relocation to rooms on the next floor up. In many homes, certain belongings do hover about in transit from time to time, but if your staircase has become a regular dumping ground, a much better solution would surely be to work out why this keeps happening – for example, are the items in question being stored too far away from where they are being used? – than to buy something that simply contributes to the clutter.

To be workable, all systems should be personal to some degree. Order is merely a way of arranging things so that they can be used in the most effective way; this is why you do not find tins and jars organized alphabetically in most kitchen cupboards. Storage systems, from fitted kitchen units to flat-pack bookshelves, offer standardized modules of space that often require customization to be of any use at all.

Some of the best storage solutions are often the simplest; peg rails and coat hooks keep outdoor gear accessible and orderly. This slightly more eccentric version has 'pegs' made from beachstones tied on to a pole with twine (above). **Hand and bath towels hanging on a plain wooden rail or suits neatly lined up along a metal, shop-style fitting are arrangements that look good as well as being practical.**

Keeping possessions behind closed doors is one solution to the problem of order. Floor-to-ceiling cupboards provide integrated, seamless storage, but visual pleasure can also be derived from organized display, whether behind glazed doors, in open units or on shelves.

With units, this might entail interior shelves spaced at different intervals and of different depths, or pull-out trays or baskets. With shelving, adjustment should be possible to accommodate the different heights, weights and sizes of books.

Order may mean clearing out everything surplus to requirements or, as in the case of Min Hogg's scissors, having a surplus of some items so they are always to hand. Equally, it can rest simply in those lateral inspirations that keep life running smoothly. Min keeps a large notebook beside the telephone, where she can note down the sort of minor domestic detail (the boiler mender's phone number and so on) that tends to get scribbled on scraps of paper and promptly lost. She dates the page and files the notebooks once they are filled – a small practicality that saves time and duplicated effort. But the value of the exercise is not merely practical; the notebooks are bound in red velvet, offering daily pleasure on this little level.

cook

The restaurant kitchen is one of the most rigorously planned of all working spaces and we can learn a great deal from its organization. There are fewer environments where the conditions are more extreme: intense heat, sharp implements and the incredible bustle of people intent on filling orders in the shortest possible time mean that precision planning is required to avoid potential disaster. In a well-planned restaurant kitchen, the layout of services and appliances is firmly based on the logic of working sequences and all necessary equipment is closely integrated with the preparation areas where they will be used.

The kitchen in your home is unlikely to see such a ferment of activity, but it is only common sense to arrange fittings and fixtures so that they follow a natural progression. You should be able to move from fridge to sink to preparation area to stove without too much in the way of backtracking; staple ingredients and frequently used equipment should be readily to hand, easily accessible and preferably in view.

I am no Luddite but I do believe that most machines and gadgets have very little place in the domestic kitchen, where good, sharp knives and a skilled pair of hands can perform the majority of tasks infinitely better and quicker. Chefs are passionate about their knives; every cook should invest in the best they can afford and keep them sharpened and properly stored in a rack or block.

Cooking in a kitchen that has been properly planned should be a little like driving a car; you should be able to reach for the salt or a spoon as instinctively as you would engage the clutch before changing gear.

Restaurant kitchens have had another impact on the way we live, which is the increasing trend for professional catering appliances and equipment to be bought for the home. Anyone who seriously enjoys cooking is bound to appreciate good, robust equipment that is capable of withstanding heavy use and is designed to the highest performance standards. At the same time, a vast *batterie de cuisine*, no matter how professional it is, will not make you a better cook. I would agree with Elizabeth David that 'too much equipment is, if anything, worse than too little', and can be the tell-tale sign of pretentiousness rather than culinary expertise.

According to John Torode, 'the easiest way to cook is to get yourself a wok and a cleaver and away you go.' After all, you can fry, boil and steam in a wok and a cleaver is just as good at dicing shallots as it is at cracking crabs. Like all chefs, he has acquired his fair share of kitchen gadgets and machines, often as presents, but they are rarely used. What does get used, however, is equipment that is directly related to his particular style of cooking. For example, he has six pestle and mortars, each with different abrasive qualities; these include a marble one for grinding peppercorns and salt crystals, a large granite one for making curry pastes, one used solely for grinding up turmeric and a thin, deep wooden one for pounding away at dry spices.

If people have a tendency to succumb to catering status symbols, they are also often seduced by 'quick-fix' kitchen gadgets. From the nifty little items that promise to halve the time and effort taken to chop carrots to the expensive, heavily accessorized machines that really only come into their own when a dozen people are expected for supper, gadgets are rarely truly necessary if you have a good range of utensils and cookware. It is far better to invest your money in high quality, sharp knives, heavy-gauge stainless-steel saucepans and cast-iron casseroles that will provide years and years of dependable use. Nothing beats the humble wooden spoon,

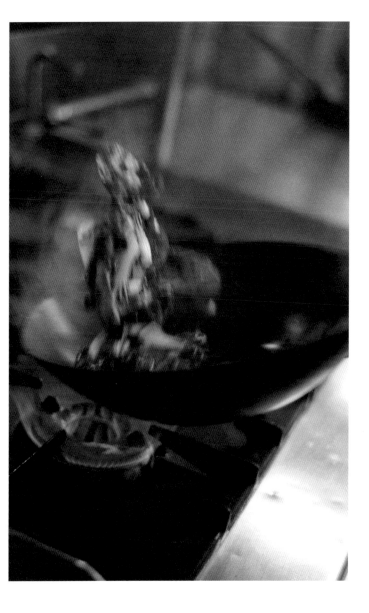

Who needs packet food when there are so many ways of cooking that are fast and simple? Stir-frying over a high heat in a wok is one of the quickest and most direct methods, and can be adapted for any number of different ingredients. Fresh shellfish, one of the most delicious of all tastes, needs little in the way of elaborate preparation or cooking.

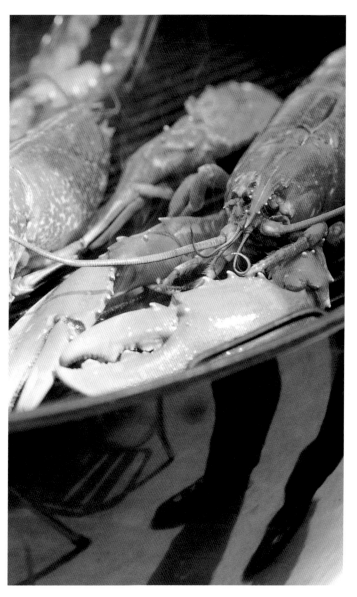

One of my favourite cooking methods is grilling – the results are even more delicious when you cook and eat outside.

While the restaurant kitchen, with its gleaming stainless-steel surfaces and racks of equipment, has had an undoubted influence on contemporary kitchen design, good quality pots, pans, baking dishes and casseroles and a basic range of utensils are all that most people really need.

stainless-steel balloon whisk or pestle and mortar, and such necessities have changed very little for generations.

Whatever you collect beyond the range of such essential tools should reflect what you like to cook, which in turn should reflect what you like to eat. If you love oriental food, it makes sense to have a wok; a pasta-maker might come in handy if you are a devotee of Italian cooking. Apart from such exceptions, basic kitchen equipment is all most of us really need. It is not only tried and tested, but it offers precisely that down-to-earth quality that makes cooking so pleasurable and rewarding in the first place.

Coping with the bare minimum in holiday homes can provide a vivid illustration of this point. Suzie Slesin has been taking holidays on the same small Greek island for many years. Her tiny house, generally filled to bursting with family and friends, has the most rudimentary facilities: cooking (on two small hot plates) always takes place outside; ingredients come from the relatively narrow range of produce the island

Kitchen style should arise
naturally out of the integrity of
the materials used for surfaces
and finishes. This old-fashioned
French kitchen has a simple,
cheerful domesticity.

has to offer; equipment is improvised. Every year she sets herself the challenge of cooking at least one meal that everyone can eat together – and what might seem superficially a vexing and frustrating exercise always proves hugely enjoyable.

As the *batterie de cuisine* as status symbol reveals, kitchen style and aesthetics can have more to do with impressing the neighbours than true ease of use or basic functionalism. In this idiom, you get kitchens designed to resemble high-tech laboratories, gleaming stainless-steel temples of hygiene and soulless efficiency, or, at the opposite end of the spectrum, kitchens decked out in all manner of pseudo-Edwardian accoutrements, with appliances concealed behind bespoke wooden panels laden with twiddly decorative mouldings. Elizabeth David had her own predictably tart views on the subject: 'I recoil from coloured tiles and beflowered surfaces and I don't want a lot of things coloured avocado and tangerine. I'll just settle for the avocados and tangerines in a bowl on the dresser. In other words, if the food and cooking pots don't provide enough visual interest and create their own changing patterns in a kitchen, then there's something wrong.'

If you keep practicality and the working nature of the kitchen in mind, style will look after itself. More than any other area in the home, kitchen surfaces and finishes have jobs to do. They must be robust enough to stand wear, resistant to extremes of heat, steam and water, easy to clean and non-slip. In many people's eyes, this might constitute an argument in favour of synthetic materials, laminate worktops, vinyl flooring and the like. I think, however, that artificial materials are, if anything, more depressing in the kitchen than anywhere else, where they jar uncomfortably with the vitality of taste, flavour and aroma that good cooking is all about. A certain hysterical paranoia about hygiene lies behind many decisions to substitute synthetics for the real thing, but it is often an unwarranted and misinformed anxiety. Linoleum, for example, a wholly natural product, actually scores higher as an anti-bacterial material than vinyl, and looks, ages and performs infinitely better. Slate shelves and stone floors provide a natural degree of refrigeration for larders and pantries; wooden worktops, butcher's blocks and chopping boards acquire a delicious aroma after years of contact with the pungent flavours of garlic, onion and ginger, a smell that is as pleasing as their visual patina.

Time and distance are built into the whole experience of cooking today. Instead of the daily stroll through the local market, there is the weekly shop at the superstore. Food is chilled, frozen or held in stock until we can no longer really remember the impulse of appetite that made us buy it in the first place. Cooking areas outside, where you can recapture the unaffected simplicity of the outdoor trattoria or taverna, and vegetable patches, fruit trees and herb gardens, where you can harvest minutes before you eat, remind us how pleasurable it is when the journey from plough to plate is very much shorter. It is this immediacy that spells easy living to me.

Eating in the kitchen, unthinkable in polite circles a half-century ago, preserves the sense of immediacy that good, simple cooking is all about.

eat

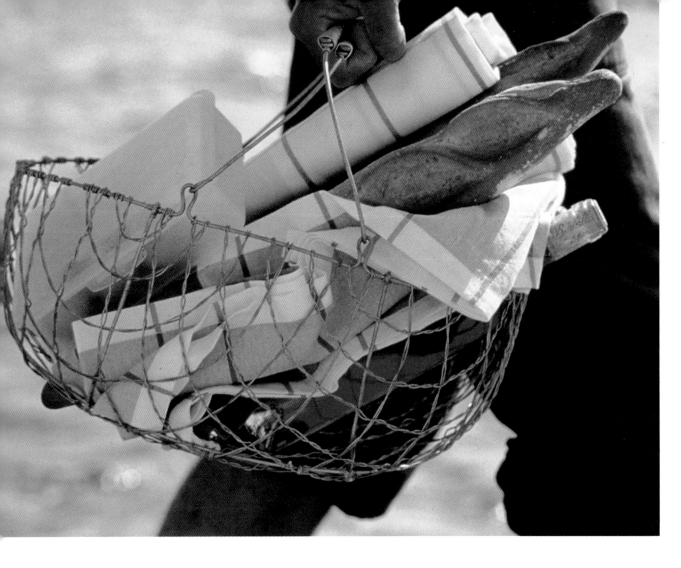

Eating outdoors is one of life's greatest pleasures – and you don't need a fully accessorized picnic hamper so stuffed with matching crockery that there is little room left for anything else – a simple basket will do. Failing that, an open doorway or even an open window, preferably looking out on to a garden, brings the same sense of vitality to indoor eating.

If you ever want to feel hungry, I suggest you read *The Wind in the Willows* by Kenneth Grahame. There is a great deal of eating in that book, much of it outdoors. The Rat's 'fat, wicker luncheon-basket' was not laden down with matching sets of crockery and cutlery but cold chicken,'coldtonguecoldham coldbeefpickledgherkinssaladfrenchrollscresssandwidges pottedmeatgingerbeerlemonadesodawater–', while the simple picnic he prepared for the adventuring Sea Rat, who sometimes woke up crying when he dreamed of 'the shell-fish of Marseilles', consisted of 'a yard of long French bread, a sausage out of which the garlic sang, some cheese which lay down and cried, and a long-necked straw-covered flask containing bottled sunshine . . . .' Perfect easy living.

Judging by the lovingly detailed descriptions of breakfasts, lunches and high teas that litter the book, from the first picnic on the river to the lobster salad supper at Toad Hall, Kenneth Grahame obviously enjoyed food very much. And as he was evidently aware, food tastes even better when you're sitting in a grassy spot with dappled light coming through the trees, or in a sheltered cove beside the sea with the waves gently crashing on the beach. One of the most memorable and most comfortable meals of my life took place one evening on a beach in the south of France. We sat eating round a big table, scrunching bare toes into the soft, warm sand while a huge crackling bonfire fuelled by broken beach chairs threw fantastic shapes into the night sky. Even the couscous tasted delicious.

Unfortunately, such experiences do not come along very often, but when they do, they illustrate the profound effect that our surroundings can have on our enjoyment of food.

As a restaurateur, I know how important the setting can be. It isn't merely a question of atmosphere. The dishes, jugs, glasses, plates and the knives and forks you use, the chairs you sit on and the table you sit at are the more functional sides of the matter. Eating itself is not really a function, of course, except in the prosaic sense of refuelling, but it does involve the consideration of certain practical factors that can significantly enhance, or undermine, what is one of the most basic of pleasures. Cooking takes care of what you eat; how and where are just as important.

I personally enjoy eating in a room that is open to other activities. In my house in the country, the kitchen is located in what was once a snooker room and there is plenty of space for a big table adjoining the area where the actual cooking takes place. It is certainly the most used room in the house.

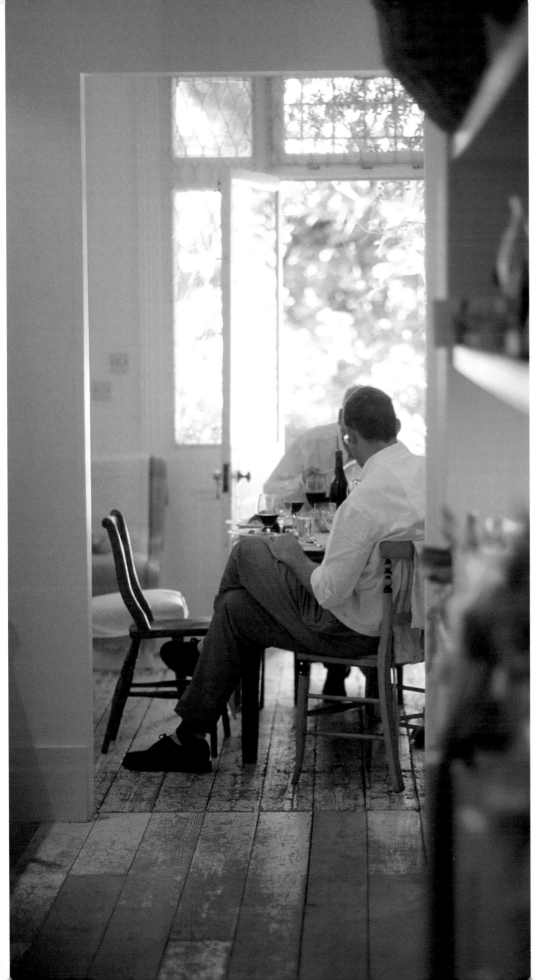

In my apartment in London, cooking, eating and living areas flow into one another in an open-plan arrangement. Eating, I believe, is at its best when it is a communal experience and multi-function spaces help to promote a sense of generosity and hospitality. And when it isn't a communal experience, when you are eating alone, it is much more pleasant to do so in a space that is integrated with the rest of the home. A separate dining room, on the other hand, is a faintly ridiculous, if not miserable, place to munch your way through a solitary supper, which is why people who have separate dining rooms tend to have more easy-going eating areas in the kitchen as well.

I am far from unusual in my tastes; the dining room as a separate entity is on the wane, as it has been ever since entertaining gained a new informality in the 1960s. Nowadays, as a relic from more hierarchical times, a separate dining room can convey a rather ponderous sense of occasion, which is at odds with everyday mealtimes. Gone are the days (in most households, anyway) when the 'little woman' toiled behind a closed kitchen door while guests sipped indifferent sherry in the drawing room waiting for the summons to sit at the dining table – where they would find, no doubt, the seating plan enshrined on neat little place cards. Ever since the kitchen door first opened, wafting out tantalizing aromas and the excited hubbub of activity, it has never really closed again. The conviviality of supper round a table within reach of the stove and second helpings, and the refusal to stand on ceremony define social customs today.

I could choose to have a separate dining room if I wished – in fact, in the country I do have one, but it is rarely used. But for most people, such an arrangement is simply an inefficient and unaffordable use of space, since for much of the time the dining room stands empty. When such high demands are placed on every square inch of our homes, the separate dining room begs to be annexed for some harder-working purpose and it often isn't long before it is. What is equally unsatisfactory is the type of atmosphere that tends to be generated by leaving a room unoccupied for much of the day. Like all underused spaces, dining rooms can

The finesse of porcelain, smooth as an eggshell, adds a sense of refinement and delicacy to the table. I also enjoy the no-nonsense functionalism of Duralex tumblers, which are perfect for the job as well as being virtually unbreakable.

stubbornly resist the attempt to bring them to life; something of a dead quality always seems to linger. Suzie Slesin, who likes to entertain quite large numbers of people at a moment's notice, has a separate dining room to make this possible, but she has kept the space alive by fitting it out as a library. Books create a companionable, clubby background for eating and when the room is not serving its dedicated function, it can be used as a place for work and study.

An open-plan arrangement, however, does not mean that activities literally have to run into each other. Eating requires a different mood from cooking and there must be some separation between the two. You need to be able to pull out your chair without crashing into a wall, or serve a meal without winding your way round obstacles. At the same time, when you actually sit down to eat you need the intimacy of the table, the closed circle of companionship, with reminders of other functions fading into the background. Dining areas need some clear space, both physically and mentally.

L-shaped areas or those converted from two former rooms offer a natural division of space. Alternatively, you can position the table within the embrace of a bay window, or on the other side of a half-height counter that serves as a partial screen for kitchen activities.

Lighting plays a huge role in creating the right atmosphere. Dimmable background light, combined with small downlights focused on the table, provide a versatile arrangement for eating – provided you do not intend to alter the position of the table at some future date. A row of small pendent lights can also be effective, but you must take care to ensure that the actual light sources are either shielded in some way or recessed deep enough within the fittings so as not to cause glare. Lighting the table properly means using the surface as a gentle form of reflection, so that diners are not dazzled or oppressed by a relentless overhead glare. Light bounced off the table to light people from below is the most flattering form of illumination.

Basic comfort and ease demands a sturdy table that is big enough for everyone to sit round, and chairs that are stable, supportive and at the right height. Highly polished or

In tableware, I am attracted to clean lines and simple forms. Teapots and jugs should pour properly, cups feel right when you grip the handle and plates sit evenly on the table.

veneered finishes, such as the mahogany acreage of the traditional formal table, do not spell easy living to me: one watermark or fingerprint and the furniture wax has to come out again. Nor am I particularly fond of glass in this context (much as I love glass). Glass tables, when they are used for eating rather than display, can have a distinctly edgy quality which some people find as uncomfortable as the sound of fingernails drawn across a blackboard. Scrubbed oak, or some other good quality hardwood make infinitely more tolerant surfaces and do not require constant vigilance. Such tables are good-looking in their own right but robust enough to do duty as a place where homework can be tackled between mealtimes. In the same way, it is important to pay attention to the way dining chairs feel when you sit on them. Surprisingly, plenty of people don't. Chairs chosen on the basis of appearance alone can often make you want to leave the table faster than lumps in the sauce or a droning bore on your left. But comfort does not have to be taken to excess – people often forget that you lean forward when you eat, so you don't need a deeply padded back rest.

Tableware has long been the focus of much snobbery and status-seeking, with elaborate dinner services embellished with gilt and rampant patterns of fruit and vegetables featuring on many wedding lists. But plates that are fancier and more colourful than the food on them seem to miss the point. Real luxury for me comes from the quality of materials and the skill employed in their manufacture. White porcelain, for example, is absolutely right for the job and a pleasure to use. Smooth, so there are no grating sounds from knife or fork; thin, to provide a sense of finesse; and unadorned to keep the attention where it belongs – on the food – such tableware has an inherent feeling of quality, not a self-proclaimed price tag. I also enjoy the sort of robust crockery you find in restaurants and cafés, not the gritty rusticity of earthenware which is much too rough to eat off comfortably, but simple basic plates and dishes that are more likely to bounce than break if you drop them. Similarly, I like both plain, thin wine glasses, tapered and shaped to deliver the bouquet to your nose, and the down-to-earth quality of chunky Duralex tumblers – forms that are firmly based on

Some form of shade is vital for outdoor eating areas, especially in a hot climate. This canvas awning (far left) gives protection from the sun and has an appropriately nautical flavour for a balcony overlooking the sea.

The presentation of food should whet the appetite, not trumpet one's status. Simple containers, plain crockery, a white cloth and properly weighted cutlery allow the food you are serving to take centre stage.

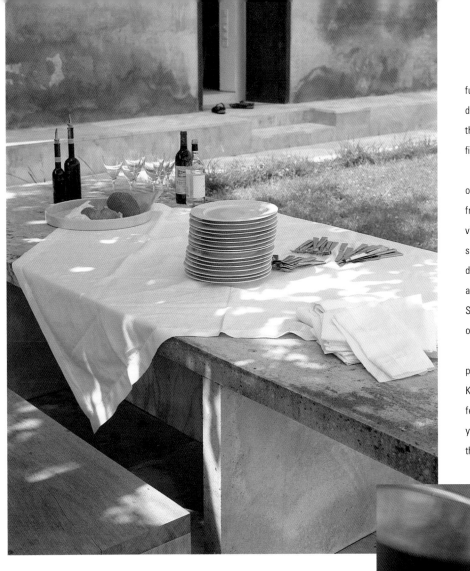

function, just as the insulating thickness of a coffee cup is designed to maintain the heat of a drink we sip slowly, and the eggshell delicacy of a teacup helps to cool a drink we find more thirst-quenching.

I am not such a purist that I would forswear all touches of colour: a blue rim on a plate, for example, can sharpen and freshen the whole look, and patterns that add a feeling of vitality without dominating can also be very attractive. Strong solid colours can provide unbeatable accents on the table: a deep indigo bowl makes a pile of lemons or limes come alive; a tomato salad on a fresh green plate is incredibly appetizing. Such jolts of contrast heighten our awareness of food – think of Elizabeth David's Venetian market.

Utensils and cutlery when they are well designed provide a small satisfaction whenever we encounter them. Knives and forks should be weighted and balanced so they feel physically right in the hand, neither so light and flimsy you feel as if you can't put pressure on them, nor so heavy that you notice the effort of picking them up. It should be easy

Fresh food, simply served from the oven or grill to the table creates a welcome immediacy of experience.

Eating should be a convivial activity, where people relax and enjoy the company as much as what they eat. I much prefer plain white porcelain, generously proportioned, to patterned dinner services that are more colourful than the food.

to pour from a jug or teapot without splashing or dripping; the angle of a ladle should match the curving action of your wrist. These may seem like small points – details – but a sense of ease and enjoyment depends on them.

There is pleasure in basic contact with food, whether you are choosing it, preparing it or eating it. John Torode believes that 'if you plan too much, everything will end up too stilted', and that it is much better to go to the market with an open mind and allow yourself to become inspired by what is fresh and in season. I agree with him entirely and practise this principle wherever possible. From that selection process of touching and looking to cooking and eating, the important thing is to keep a relaxed attitude. When he has friends for supper, he puts big pots of food in the middle of the table and big spoons for people to help themselves. Crockery is deep white plates from a seconds' shop and Japanese noodle bowls; cutlery is plain bone-handled knives and forks bought in bundles from a market stall. 'I don't think we even have a tablecloth,' he says. 'It's a matter of sitting back and enjoying it. And the enjoyment comes from conversation and people as much as the food that brings them together.'

work

A dedicated work room is more or less essential if you are pursuing a career from home, but there is no need to import the office aesthetic. A wall of shelving provides systematic organization for books and files in a spacious work room (above). **In my study at home in London, rows of closely hung prints of brushes and tools put me in the mood for work** (above centre).

Lack of distraction owes as much to a certain simplicity of surroundings as it does to seclusion of location. Dahl's writing shed, where he worked sitting under heaps of blankets in cold weather with a drawing board on his lap and copious supplies of chocolate to hand, was more eccentric and perhaps more basic than most, but arranging things to suit yourself is the point at issue. Philippe Starck is one person I know who also finds he is at his most creative and productive when he deliberately puts himself in a position where he lives very simply. Focusing on the task at hand becomes easier when other layers of life are peeled away.

Escaping to the garden or shed is one way of working at home. For more organized home businesses, a slightly more professional version of the shed idea may be necessary to provide clients with a separate access that does not offer unwelcome glimpses of your domestic life. A dedicated work room or area can be particularly important if your livelihood depends upon it. In an office, it is easy enough to kid yourself that simply being there in some way constitutes working. With no one to call time on your coffee breaks, or monitor your personal phone calls, or point out that weeding the vegetable patch may be work but it isn't the same as completing the order by next Tuesday, lack of distraction can make all the difference between sinking and swimming. A work room or study won't make you self-disciplined all by itself, but it will close the door on peripheral temptations.

But with separate rooms in short supply in most households, some form of integration of home and working life is inevitable for many people. The question is how you achieve the same quality of concentration when you must work in areas that also serve other purposes. When work space shrinks to desk space, you need to be able to set up some form of psychological barrier between yourself and the rest of the home, which means choosing a location where interruptions are less likely and every square inch of space is not in competition from other activities: such as an alcove in a living area, a dining area between mealtimes or a workspace created from part of a bedroom. Where an area is devoted to different activities, a physical separation, such

as a screen, divider or a half-width partition, can make a lot of difference, creating a suggestion of enclosure which provides room for thought. But perhaps the most important element is a desk or bureau that can expand while you are working, then swallow up your work when you close it down.

The joy of working from home is that it offers the opportunity to create an environment that is personal, congenial and comfortable, instead of one that displays the same lowest-common-denominator functionalism you left behind with the numbered parking space and key to the executive washroom. As working from home becomes more of a social trend and less of a euphemism for skiving off, there is also an increasing need to reconcile the professional with

A study at home can be a spare room, an attic, a basement or a converted garage – ideally out of the main run of things. The point is to tailor the space to create the right working conditions for you. This studio (above), **with tables arranged to benefit from the natural light, provides room for the personal touches discouraged in most offices.**

If you don't have enough room for a separate study or home office, space will need to be found in an area where other activities take place. In such instances, the right conditions are even more important to gain the necessary psychological separation from the rest of the household.

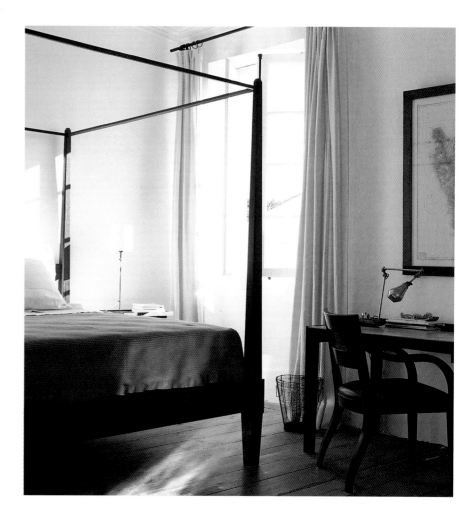

A desk placed at a window, so that you sit with your back to the rest of the room, is one arrangement that can help concentration. A comfortable chair to support your back and at the right height for the work surface is essential.

the domestic: spreading your papers over the kitchen table or parking your pens in an empty tin with the label soaked off might do for a while, but eventually you need to show you mean business – if only to yourself. How you arrange and equip your workspace and the accessories you choose to accompany it can help to bridge the gap between the home-in-the-office and the office-in-the-home.

Work that is primarily desk-bound may not require much in the way of surrounding space beyond what is required to house files, books, papers and other supplies. But the quality of the immediate working area is critical. Decent light, both natural and artificial, a comfortable chair, a sound work surface and an infrastructure of power and phone lines are essential.

Many people equip a study or work area with cast-off office equipment or designs that share the same defiantly harsh aesthetic, an approach that may indicate they are missing the office more than they care to admit. This seems a huge pity to me, when there are so many alternatives that function just as effectively, if not more so, but offer a much higher degree of pleasure in use. A sturdy wooden table of the right height is infinitely more enjoyable to work at than a flimsy prefabricated workstation and it supplies a material dimension that helps to humanize work. At the same time, many pieces of functional equipment have an inherent rightness of design, which can be equally appealing. A well-made steel filing cabinet, which can be pushed under the table, or an Anglepoise lamp are hard-working designs with a pleasing simplicity of use and appearances that fit easily into a domestic environment.

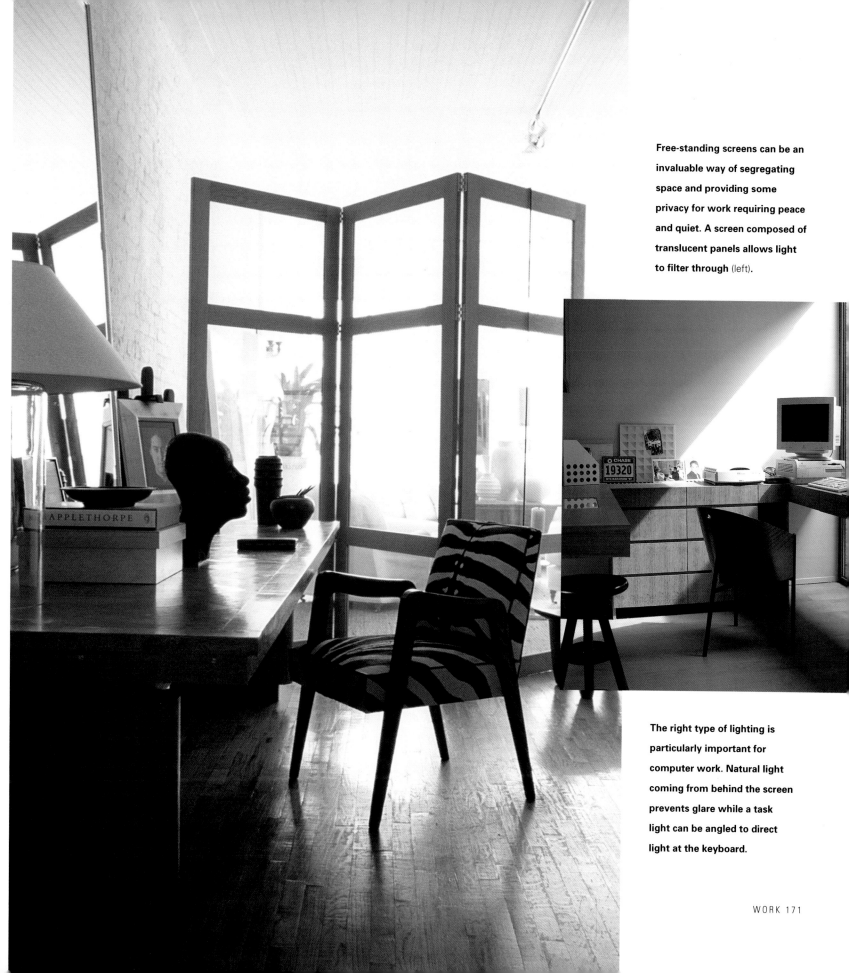

Free-standing screens can be an invaluable way of segregating space and providing some privacy for work requiring peace and quiet. A screen composed of translucent panels allows light to filter through (left).

The right type of lighting is particularly important for computer work. Natural light coming from behind the screen prevents glare while a task light can be angled to direct light at the keyboard.

When working from home, you can usually choose the level of technology that is most appropriate and productive for you. I prefer a pen with a free flow of ink or a good sharp pencil when it comes to sketching out ideas.

Equipping your own working area often means you can choose a level of technology appropriate to you rather than have someone else's idea of efficiency foisted upon you. If you miss the daily exchange of gossip by the office photocopier, console yourself with the fact that the popularity of the copier as a rendezvous stems from its propensity to break down, jam and cause queues. Easy living means reducing unnecessary frustration, which can mean revising your attitude to machines. The computer, which adds another desktop to the desktop, is essential for many types of work, but its dominance can be irritating as well as intrusive, especially where working areas are set up within more open-plan living spaces. A laptop, which is as portable as pads of paper, pens and books, may be a better solution, and can be packed away to clear the desk and mind for reading and thinking. For me, however, nothing remains as pleasurable or as productive to use as a good pen, the flow of ink in perfect response to the flow of words or ideas.

Paid work, of whatever variety, is not the only form of domestic labour. Housework must also get done, everything from washing dishes and clothes to the routine maintenance of vacuuming and dusting. Increasingly, most people's approach to such chores is to rely heavily on electrical appliances and powerful chemical cleaning products, or to pay someone else to do the work. But where does it stop? There is a new trend for 'cash-rich, time-poor' Californians to employ other people to manage virtually every aspect of their lives, from scheduling dental appointments to choosing a new house and moving all their belongings into it. The understandable aim is to save time and effort, but the result can be a frantic acceleration of life as you try to pack more and more into the day, while a mania for delegation risks turning you into little more than a house guest in your own home. Curiously, many overstressed high-fliers who go off to remote hillside farmhouses on spiritual 'retreats' frequently find that activities they would normally perceive as drudgery, such as washing up and sweeping floors, can suddenly take on an almost Zen-like significance. When the surroundings are basic and there isn't a vacuum cleaner for miles, enlightenment can take the surprising form of rediscovering the soothing quality of simple work.

Few of us are prepared to forgo modern convenience entirely, but an improved quality of living can be achieved by ensuring that the places where work must be done and the tools which we use are as decent and well designed as possible. If the kitchen has shed its dreary, neglected aesthetic in recent years, many utility areas are still in the Dark Ages. There is no reason why this should be so. A dank laundry room is a miserable place to wash clothes and linen; a crumbling cobwebbed shed full of tangled garden implements won't inspire you when it comes to spring planting. Taking care over such behind-the-scenes spaces goes a long way to putting you in the right mood for work.

Plain functional tools for indoors and out, from laundry baskets and dustpans to rakes and spades, also minimize frustration and introduce the ease that comes from pleasure of use. They feel right in the hand, they perform well and they last.

The artist's studio – with props and incidental objects to spark the imagination, brushes, paints and tools to hand and room to make a mess – is the ultimate creative working space. Drenched in natural light, this glowing room is the studio of the British artist Patrick Heron (left).

The shed is every gardener's favourite haunt. But a surprising number of artists and writers have also found the shed to be a convenient creative retreat. George Bernard Shaw's writing hut in his garden at Ayot St Lawrence sat on a rotating pedestal so that the entire shed could be swivelled round to face the sun.

By contrast, the ironing board that collapses in a shrieking metallic wheeze every time you try to put it up, or the vacuum cleaner that coughs up piles of dust, or the brush that stubbornly refuses to remain attached to its handle erode any small satisfaction one might derive from basic daily chores. The Shakers, whose dedication to work was an integral part of their religious philosophy, understood the value of good tools; their tools and fittings, from brooms to pegboards, display the same quality of loving craftsmanship that is prized in their furniture. It also helps if what you are maintaining – whether it's a tabletop or floor – is made of the type of material that does not require constant niggling vigilance and titivating to remain vaguely attractive. Real materials that age well often also clean and keep well.

Many types of work have the potential to provide a great deal of satisfaction: easy living, at times, may be less about avoiding work altogether and more about enjoying whatever you do. It is interesting that many of us choose to relax, not by lying comatose under a pile of Sunday papers, but by actively engaging in some other form of activity. Gardening, cooking, even cleaning can provide an invigorating change of gear, the chance to engage another part of the mind.

detail

In my introduction, I referred to Vita Sackville-West's list of personal pleasures, her catalogue of 'through leaves'. Detail in the home works in a similar fashion. It offers the same sort of smooth, seamless operation of a well-made drawer or well-oiled lock but it also provides flashes of pure pleasure that are no less agreeable for being unmomentous. A fleeting view from a landing window, scented flowers, light shining through coloured glass and dappling the floor – such details create a sense of place as much as the larger matters of decor and design. Their essence is surprise, and a certain transience. The view you catch out of the corner of your eye as you pass by remains intriguing far longer than the static panorama of a picture window. Fresh flowers provide more delight in the week or two of their short lives than the dried arrangements that sit ignored and dusty all year round. Detail, as the expression of personality and taste, is the heart and soul of easy living.

Details, however, can trip you up. If God is in them, so, too, is the devil. Before architects sign off new buildings, they have to undertake an often tedious fault-finding mission in which they tour the site, noting every deficiency – cracks, substandard workmanship, missing handles, unpainted guttering – so that the shortfalls can be made good before the final handover. The term for this process is 'snagging' and it describes perfectly the kind of minor aggravation that catches your attention just long enough to annoy you but, all too often, not really long enough for you to fix it. A dripping tap, a drawer that won't close properly, a loose floorboard, an overstuffed cupboard whose contents spill out every time you open the door are all 'details' that can stand in the way of easy living.

Inertia may be one reason why we put up with such vexations and put off the day when we intend to tackle them; another might be an acknowledgment of the innate awkwardness of inanimate objects, or, as in that French phrase quoted by Vita Sackville-West, *la méchanceté des choses* – the naughtiness of things. The inherent waywardness of the string that always gets tangled in the bottom of the drawer or the lid of the butter dish that always gets mislaid is closely related to the law of household perversity that states that if you take the trouble to fix one thing, two things will break the next day. Minor failures of function, however, are an inevitable side effect of use and wear; handles work loose, doors swell, paint peels off and cupboards become silted with clutter. Unlike an architect who can turn a job over to a client and hopefully be done with it, it's better to accept that in most homes 'snagging' is an on-going process. Making the effort to put small things right from time to time pays enormous dividends in making living easier.

It goes without saying that what is gimcrack, rickety and flimsy in the first place won't stand much chance of surviving even a regular dose of wear and tear. Most people are inclined to learn the hard way and this persuasive argument in favour of investing in quality at the outset, or at least in the best you can afford, seems to hit home only after you've gone the long way round.

Detail, as the hallmark of good design, is revealed in the quality of workmanship and functional performance, the degree of extra care that shows itself slowly over time. Strong, well-made hinges capable of bearing the weight of a door without buckling, the reassuring grip of handles that truly fit the hand, locked seams that delay fraying, the angle of a spout that pours right every time are not accidental presences, but the result of a thoughtful design process. Attention to this kind of detail is hugely important to me. Whether we're designing something new for the shops or buying

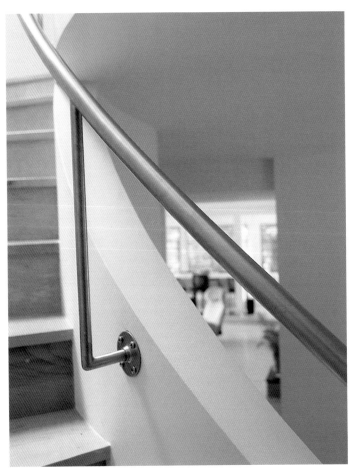

in products from elsewhere, every item is subject to the same intense scrutiny and analysis. Does it work properly? How does it feel when you hold it? Will it tip over too easily if you brush against it? Does it mark or stain too readily? Will it age gracefully? As a consumer, it is equally important to weigh alternatives and second-guess how something will work and look, not just the first time you use it, but the fifty-first time as well.

In a wider context, detail is both what you see and what you don't see. You shouldn't see pipes interrupting walls or snaking along at floor level, collecting dust and grease; neither should there be wires trailing across your path threatening to trip you up or lying in a tangled heap by an overloaded socket. It takes planning and effort to eliminate this type of unwelcome detail, but it is an essential part of getting the infrastructure of your home in order.

The interior detail with which most people are familiar is architectural or 'period': cornices, mouldings, ceiling roses, skirting boards, dado rails and architraves – the whole kit of historical parts. Interestingly, however, many such details, no matter how decorative they appear, were often originally conceived with rather more practical purposes in mind.

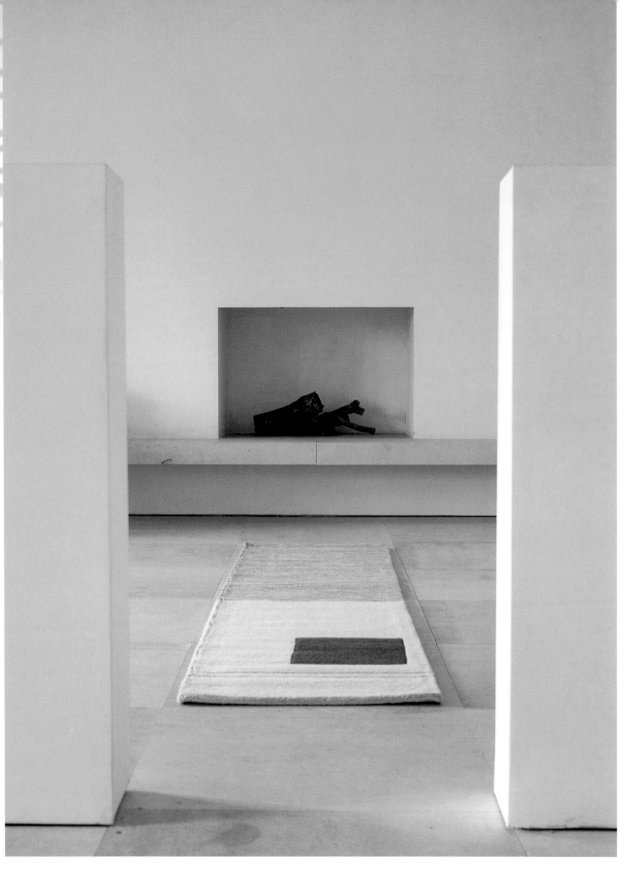

Architectural detail, in most people's minds, is synonymous with historic or period features. But it can also mean the extra degree of care taken over such seemingly minor points as edges, fittings and fixtures, switches, catches and handles. The sculptural sweep of a stair, lined in wood, relies on a precision finish; the smooth curve of a banister gives pleasure every time you use the stairs; the hearth remains a powerful focus in a contemporary space.

Everyone has their passions; one of mine is glass. Some of my collection is displayed on a table at the bottom of the stairs in my London apartment (left), top-lit by natural light spilling down from above. The fragility and translucence of certain flowers are another favourite and share similar qualities – characteristics enhanced by light.

The skirting board, for example, may appear, on a superficial level, to be a comfortable finishing touch, lending definition to the junction between the two planes of the wall and the floor. More prosaically, it exists as an acknowledgment of how extremely difficult it is to achieve a straight edge in plaster or to allow the exact margin for shrinkage or building movement; it's a cover-up, in other words. Minimalists, who prefer their walls to remain unadorned, with razor-sharp edges, will tell you how expensive and laborious it can be to do without this kind of detail. In the same way, cornicing, whether it is Georgian egg-and-dart or Victorian wedding cake, disguises the inevitable cracking that occurs where plastered wall meets plastered ceiling.

Perhaps the most cherished architectural detail of all is the fireplace. In the past, of course, it was hardly a detail, more the central practicality of the home, where food was cooked, washing water boiled and enough warmth generated to make the grind of daily life tolerable. As a gathering place or focus (the literal meaning of 'hearth'), the fireplace has long had a powerful hold on our emotions. We don't need a fireplace when we have central heating – in fact, one would have to turn the heating down to enjoy a real fire without sweltering – but huddling up to a radiator on a cold day just doesn't have the same appeal. The sight of flames flickering in the hearth or behind the glass door of a wood-burning stove adds a sense of vitality as well as a soothing reassurance; the smell of woodsmoke is one of the most evocative aromas I know, and the television is certainly no substitute.

Anything you hang on the wall, whether family photographs, a child's scribbles or leaves collected on a walk, assumes importance. A massed display has graphic impact, but casual propping on a tabletop, shelf or chest can be just as effective. Pictures hung in corners, on side or flanking walls, or where the eye glimpses them in passing, surprise and delight for longer than those on prominent display.

As people have rather belatedly come to realize, stripping away such original features is both counter-productive and unsightly. Old rooms with traces of their past surgically removed often look unbalanced and disjointed; what's missing is not merely a decorative flourish but a way of making sense of scale and proportion. The reverse – slotting off-the-peg features into a plain modern room – results in a different sense of unease. Stick-on cornices and chair rails tacked at some arbitrary point halfway up the wall may promise instant history, but no one is really fooled – architectural detail should be a natural expression of the basic character of your home.

There is another type of architectural detail that has to do with finesse. The banister that is uninterrupted by clumsy supports, so your hand can slide smoothly all the way from top to bottom, is as lovely to touch as it is to look at. The neat finish where two different types of flooring meet is both practical – preventing materials from lifting or chipping – and visually pleasing. The extra attention paid to minor points, such as socket and switch covers, door knobs and catches, invests everything with a feeling of thoughtfulness and care.

At the same time, detail is all about pleasure. On the level of enjoyment, it embraces wit, surprise and personal expression: the imagination in free play. Things that exist purely for their own sake – a bowl of lemons, a bunch of fragrant flowers, photographs of family and friends, and paintings – add pure joy in small doses and life would be much poorer without them.

Some of the most evocative objects are handmade. Handblown glass, for example, possesses none of the mechanical uniformity of a factory product, but retains a hint of the organic fluidity of molten glass itself. Similarly, handthrown pots express the plasticity of raw clay, the sense in which the material shapes what you can do with it. In the slight irregularity of appearance and feel, such objects connect us directly with the process of making. You can almost see the intuitive choreography of the glassblower or feel the centrifugal force of the wheel pulling on the potter's hands. When so much else in the world comes off a production line, we need such reminders of human creativity around us.

Working detail makes the difference between life running smoothly and constant frustration. It may lie in the thoughtfulness of design, such as the lipped rim of a tray that allows it to be carried more easily, the exact fitting of wooden joints or the smooth operation of well-made drawers.

Whatever you display should express a similar sense of connection. Suzie Slesin, who is incredibly well travelled, has learned to recognize those elements that are 'strong in style, that have a point of view', objects that are embedded with a sense of place and authenticity. It is not a quality that can be simulated or imposed; it's personal and comes naturally when you have the courage of your convictions, when you select what you really like and 'go to the end of your feelings'.

Works of art – from a child's drawing to a sculpture or painting – have the same ability to convey meaning and feeling. So many displays are merely dreary expressions of what people think ought to be on view: hence, the timid rows of neatly framed, mass-produced botanical prints that might as well be hanging in the corridor of a provincial hotel for all the visual pleasure they generate. If buying a work of art sounds intimidating, a pursuit only for the rich or knowledgeable museum curators, bear in mind that many original pieces are not only well within the average person's financial reach but are readily accessible in local galleries, art schools and exhibitions. Investment potential has nothing to do with it at all. There will always be gas and electricity bills to pay, mortgage interest rate rises and other

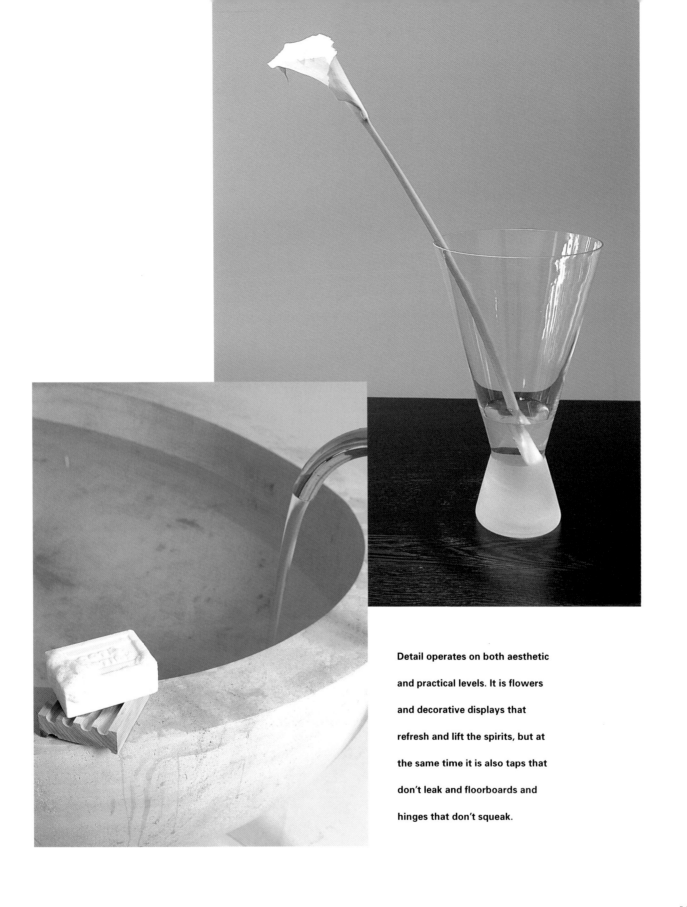

Detail operates on both aesthetic and practical levels. It is flowers and decorative displays that refresh and lift the spirits, but at the same time it is also taps that don't leak and floorboards and hinges that don't squeak.

reasons why such purchases are not strictly prudent and sensible. It takes a certain leap of faith to buy or display what really moves you, but the result will give you pleasure on a daily basis and imbue your home with your personality.

Detail can be as ephemeral as a bowl of roses, a postcard propped on the mantelpiece, a snapshot of a favourite place, something that jogs your memory. Transience is the essence of such arrangements; they come and go. Flowers are Joseph's favourite things of all; against the neutral background of his home, they provide the living accent of colour. The joy, of course, is that such accents are always changing and it is the element of surprise that keeps interiors alive.

Massed in a simple container, on the desk, on the dining table, by the bedside, flowers lift the spirits like nothing else. I can think of nothing more likely to generate a mood of optimism than a vase full of white roses: beautiful form, generous simplicity and a gentle, instantly recognizable perfume.

The most important details of all are those that make your home yours and not anyone else's. They are the things that remind you of where you've been, what you've done, whom you've known and loved. They are the things that, if your house was on fire, your insurance was paid up and your family was safe, you would rescue. The close focus of detail identifies what makes life truly worth living.

The least inspiring displays are composed of objects you expect to see, or those that remain in the same dusty corner year after year. By contrast, objects that mean something to you, that enshrine memories of a favourite place or time or person, always have vitality: they actually have something to say. You can group objects by type, colour or texture, but there really are no hard-and-fast rules for display except to surround yourself with things you positively enjoy.

acknowledgments

The publisher thanks the following photographers and organizations for their kind permission to reproduce the photographs in this book:

2–3 Verne Fotografie; 5 above left Stuart McIntyre/Lene Utzon (Architect: Alex Popov); 5 above centre Verne Fotografie; 8–9 left Robert Mort; 9 above left Ingalill Snitt; 9 below right Mirjam Bleeker/Frank Visser & Taverne Agency; 10 both pictures Mirjam Bleeker/Frank Visser & Taverne Agency; 11 left William Meppem/Vogue Entertaining; 12 left Ingalill Snitt; 12 right Mirjam Bleeker/Frank Visser & Taverne Agency; 12–13 Neo Vision/Photonica; 13 above right Mirjam Bleeker/ Frank Visser & Taverne Agency ; 13 below Andrew Wood/ The Interior Archive (courtesy of Douglas Johnson); 14 above left Herbert Ypma/The Interior Archive (Architect: Yturbe); 14 below David Loftus/Vogue Entertaining; 15–16 Carlos Navajas; 18 Verne Fotografie (D. Jasiack); 20 Stuart McIntyre/ Lene Utzon (Architect: Alex Popov); 21 Stuart McIntyre/Lene Utzon (Architect: Alex Popov); 22 Marie Pierre-Morel/Marie Claire Maison; 23 Belle Magazine; 26 Edina van der Wyck/ The Interior Archive (Architect: Sophie Hicks); 27 left Luke White/Axiom Photographic Agency (Le Corbusier © FLC/ ADAGP, Paris and DACS, London 1999); 27 above right Britstock-IFA/West Stock/Peterson; 27 below right David Gamble; 29 left Jan Verlinde; 29 above right Belle Magazine; 30 left Tim Rainger (Architect: Andrew Patterson, New Zealand); 30 right Mark Luscombe-Whyte (Le Corbusier, Sarabhai house, India © FLC/ADAGP, Paris and DACS, London 1999); 31 Mark Luscombe-Whyte (Le Corbusier, Sarabhai house, India © FLC/ADAGP, Paris and DACS, London 1999); 32 above left Mark Luscombe-Whyte; 32 above centre Verne Fotografie (Sestig); 32 below Jan Verlinde; 33 below Belle Magazine; 36 left Verne Fotografie; 37 Jorn Stjerneklar/Impact; 39 John Gollings; 41 below Yuri Dojc/The Image Bank; 42 left Ingalill Snitt; 42 right Eigenhuis and Interieur/Hotze Eisma; 44 above left D. Vorillon/Inside (Architect: Biben-Bosley); 44 below left Deidi von Schaewen (Asilah Dubois); 44 below right Deidi von Schaewen (Asilah Dubois); 44–45 main picture Dennis Gilbert/View (Architect: Peter Romaniuk); 45 below Verne Fotografie; 48–49 above Ken/Photonica; 50 above left Francesco Venturi; 50 centre David Loftus/Vogue Entertaining; 51 G.I. Bernard/Natural History Photographic Agency; 52 left David Loftus/Vogue Entertaining; 52–53 main picture Michael Mack; 53 right David Loftus/Vogue Entertaining; 54 above Peter Margonelli; 54 below William Meppem/Vogue Entertaining; 58 above Mark Luscombe-Whyte; 59 Paul Ryan/International Interiors (Architect: David Ling); 60 above Craig Fraser/Stylist: Shelley Street (Architects: Richard Tremeer and Jon Jacobson); 60 below Sainsbury's The Magazine/Peter Knab; 61 left W. Thompson/Photonica; 62 left Verne Fotografie (Terence Conran); 62 right Nicolas Tosi/Stylist: Marion Bayle/Marie Claire Maison; 63 Verne Fotografie (Hans Verstuuyft); 64 Mark Luscombe-Whyte (Le Corbusier, Sarabhai house, India

© FLC/ADAGP, Paris and DACS, London 1999); 65 above Ingalill Snitt; 65 below right David George; 66–67 Geoff Howard/Camera Press; 70 Gentl & Hyers/Photonica; 71 Conran Collection/photography by Earl Carter; 74 George Seper/Vogue Entertaining; 76 Earl Carter/Belle/Arcaid; 77 above R.C. Stradtmann/Schöner Wohnen/Camera Press; 77 below Eric Morin; 78 Verne Fotografie (Koningshank); 79 Simon Kenny/Vogue Living; 80 above left Mirjam Bleeker/Frank Visser & Taverne Agency; 80 below I. Vanderharst/Robert Harding Picture Library; 80–81 Mads Mogensen; 81 below Minh + Wass; 82 Richard Bryant/Arcaid (Gwathmey Siegel Architects); 83 above Stuart McIntyre/Lene Utzon (Architect: Alex Popov); 86 left Alan Evrard/Impact; 88 Marie Pierre-Morel/Stylist: Catherine Ardouin/Marie Claire Maison; 89 left Annabel Elston/World of Interiors; 89 right Hannah Lewis/Homes & Gardens/Robert Harding Syndication; 90 above right Conran Collection/photography by Earl Carter; 91 Minh + Wass; 93 above right Verne Fotografie (Pentogram, NY); 93 below Verity Welstead; 97 Eigenhuis and Interieur/Hotze Eisma; 98–99 Verne Fotografie (Barbara Bin); 100 above right Marie Pierre-Morel/Marie Claire Maison; 100–101 Mark Darley/Esto; 101 Alexander van Berge; 102 right Roland Beauffre/Agence Top; 102 above Stuart McIntyre/Lene Utzon (Architect: Alex Popov); 102 below left Conran Collection/photography by Earl Carter; 103 Earl Carter/Belle/Arcaid; 104–105 Nicolas Tosi/Stylist: Catherine Ardouin/Marie Claire Maison; 105 Gilles de Chabaneix/Stylist: Catherine Ardouin/Marie Claire Maison; 106 Sakio Komiya/© Kateigaho; 107 left Verne Fotografie; 110 left Scott Faulkner; 110 below Hotze Eisma; 112 left Maison Madame Figaro/N.Tosi; 112 right Andrew Wood/The Interior Archive (Bali); 113 above left Verne Fotografie; 113 below Stuart McIntyre/Lene Utzon (Architect: Alex Popov); 114–115 Deidi von Schaewen (Le Corbusier, Sarabhai house, India © FLC/ADAGP, Paris and DACS, London 1999); 117 above Conran Collection/ photography by Earl Carter; 117 below Diana Miller/Conran Octopus; 118 Jan Verlinde; 119 left Christian Sarramon; 120–121 Geoff Howard/Camera Press; 124 Maura McEvoy; 125 Petrina Tinsley/Vogue Entertaining; 128 Belle Magazine; 129 Hotze Eisma ; 130–131 Verity Welstead; 132 above left Verity Welstead; 132 above right W. Waldron/Inside (Maison Alison Spear, NY); 132 below J. Hay/Vogue Living; 133 Jan Verlinde; 134 left Paul Ryan/International Interiors (Eugenie Voorhees); 135 left Tim Beddow/World of Interiors; 135 right Penelope Chauvelot/Stylist: Michèle Bocquillon/Marie France; 137 above Verne Fotografie (Vincent van Duysen, Belgium); 140 above Conran Restaurants; 140 below Mads Mogensen; 141 James Mortimer/©Johnny Grey; 142 left Conran Restaurants; 142 all pictures Yves Duronsoy; 144 left Georgie Cole/Vogue Entertaining; 144 right Verne Fotografie; 145 above left William Meppem/Vogue Entertaining ; 145 above right Earl Carter/Vogue Entertaining; 145 below Jan Baldwin; 146 left Octopus Publishing Group Ltd/Sandra Lane; 148–149 Andrew Wood/The Interior Archive (David Edgeall); 149 right Huntley

Hedworth (Designed by: © Jane Taylor & Andrew Parr, tel. 0171 499 7101); 150 left Pia Tryde/Conran Restaurants; 150 right Alexandre Baillache/Stylist: Catherine Ardouin/ Marie Claire Maison; 151 Stuart McIntyre/Lene Utzon (Architect: Alex Popov); 154 Habitat UK; 155 Nicolas Bruant/Homes & Gardens/Robert Harding Syndication; 156 left Maura McEvoy; 156 right Geoff Lung/Vogue Entertaining; 158 left Deidi von Schaewen (Dorget, Morocco); 158–159 Maura McEvoy; 159 above Maura McEvoy; 159 below right Zimmermann's/Stylist: Gerd Sommerlade/Elle Decoration, Germany; 161 below left Food Illustrated /Diana Miller; 161 below right Geoff Lung/Vogue Entertaining; 162 below Conran Collection/photography by Earl Carter; 166 left Jan Verlinde; 166 right Andrew Wood/The Interior Archive; 168 left Jan Verlinde; 168–169 Verne Fotografie; 169 right Earl Carter/Vogue Entertaining; 170 left Edina van der Wyck/The Interior Archive; 170 right Paul Ryan/International Interiors (Designer: Christian Liaigre); 171 left Marie Pierre-Morel/Stylist: Daniel Rozensztroch/Marie Claire Maison; 172–173 Andrew Wood/The Interior Archive (Jérôme Abel Seguin); 174 left C. Simon Sykes/The Interior Archive; 174–175 right C. Simon Sykes/The Interior Archive (© Patrick Heron. All rights reserved, DACS 1998); 175 right Howard Rice; 178 left Richard Bryant/Arcaid (Architects: Tsao & McKown); 178 right Paul Ryan/International Interiors (Architects: Hariri & Hariri); 180 Sakio Komiya/© Kateigaho; 181 left Conran Collection/photography by Earl Carter; 181 right Nicolas Tosi/Stylist: Marion Bayle/Marie Claire Maison; 182 centre Marie Pierre Morel/Stylist: Daniel Rozenstroch/Marie Claire Maison; 182–183 Peter Margonelli ; 184 centre Mark Luscombe-Whyte; 186 Paul Ryan/International Interiors (Ivan Chermayeff); 187 left Luc Wauman; 187 right Verne Fotografie; 188 Marie Pierre Morel/Stylist: Catherine Ardouin/ Marie Claire Maison; 189 Jérôme Darblay

All other photographs specially taken for this book, © James Mitchell

The following photographs show products available from Conran Collection:

5 above right; 5 below; 28; 29 below right; 32–33; 33 above right; 36 centre; 36 right; 38 below left; 40; 41 above; 43; 50 below left; 50–51; 51 right; 55 left; 55 right; 58 below; 61 right; 65 left; 71; 75; 83 below; 89 right; 90 above right; 92 left; 100 left; 102 below left; 107 right; 110; 112; 113 left; 113 right; 117 above; 123; 136 above right; 137 below; 148 left; 157; 161 above; 162 right; 162 below; 176; 179; 181 left; 182 above left; 184 left; 185 right

Every effort has been made to trace the copyright holders; we apologize in advance for any unintentional omission and will be pleased to insert the appropriate acknowledgment in subsequent editions.